DROPSHIPPING

HOW TO LEARN ALL THE SECRETS OF DROPSHIPPING

PAUL J. ABRAMAH

Dropshipping

Paul J. Abramah

TABLE OF CONTENTS

Dropshipping

INTRODUCTION

Before you begin any business venture, it is always a good idea to know exactly what you are getting into. This way, you can make an informed choice with your time and money. Furthermore, knowing what you are getting into means that you can have an easier time actually creating your business because you know exactly what it takes to create success with that business model, which means you are more likely to be successful overall.

Instead of jumping straight into talking about how you can find products and suppliers and how to build your dropshipping business, we are going to start with the very basics. Imagine that you have never heard of dropshipping before and that you are brand new to this concept, and that you are curious about how you can legitimately turn this into a business. This way, you are able to ensure that you have a strong understanding of exactly what it is that you are about to begin creating!

To make it simple: dropshipping is a form of retail fulfillment where you have a company that is not responsible for keeping the products that it sells in its own possession. Rather than you being responsible for sourcing, purchasing, storing, shipping, and otherwise managing the products involved in your business, someone else takes care of all of this. When you sell merchandise from your store, the company responsible for your products will receive notification of the sale and fulfill the shipping for that product. They will also manage any returns or other product-related functions that need to happen in order for your business to run. You will only be responsible for paying that company for the products that you sell to your customers.

The possession of inventory and the way that inventory is managed, is the primary difference between dropshipping and standard retail companies. If you were running a standard retail company online, you would be required to purchase, store, and manage your entire inventory. This part of running a retail business can be incredibly time-consuming, as well as expensive, which is why many people do not begin retail businesses. If you can cut this part out, however, you can make the business far more sustainable while still having the capacity to earn a fairly strong income from your business. This is where dropshipping comes in, and is why dropshipping can be such a powerful way to create an income with your business.

Dropshipping is an excellent business model for just about anyone to get started with. If you are brand new to online business, if you are an entrepreneur looking to spread out your income channels, if you are looking to get into entrepreneurship but have a low budget, or if you are testing out a niche, dropshipping is excellent for you to get started with. This business model does not require a large amount of capital to start with, and it can offer a high payoff fairly quickly. If you remain consistent in your efforts and follow a proven successful strategy from the start, you can use dropshipping to help you earn more money while also learning more about the market.

CHAPTER 1

Pros & Cons of Dropshipping

D ropshipping is different from the other retails models due to this major factor - the retail owner or merchant does not own inventory or stock. The merchant instead purchases this inventory as and when it is needed from their third-party supplier that focuses on manufacturing or wholesaling, in order to meet customer demands.

In other words, dropshipping works as below:

- The customer makes an order for a product seen on the merchant's online store.
- The merchant records the order purchase and automatically sends this to the dropship supplier, complete with order details and customer information.
- The dropship supplier packages the product and ships it according to the customer's given information.

This is an extremely effective and attractive business model as it eliminates the purpose of the merchant to have a physical business venue like an office space or even a warehouse. All they ever need is internet access, a website and a device connected to the internet to upload, update and store information on their products and services if any.

Pros of Dropshipping

There are plenty of benefits to this dropshipping business model. These are:

- It is extremely easy to set up. Unlike setting up a brick-and-mortar business space, this retail model only involves just three steps which is i) finding the supplier ii) setting up a good website and once that is done iii) selling your products and services
- This model is easy to understand and implement especially for a new coming into the e-commerce industry
- To set up your business with the dropship model, the cost involved is literally next to nothing. Unlike in traditional business models where the major costs go into the setting and running of the operations, in dropshipping this step is eliminated and all the cost you need to think of is the applications you need to run your website, domain registration, hosting as well as themes you use - which is not much.
- Dropshipping risks are significantly lower because there is little to no pressure about selling inventory.
- This type of business model can be run from anywhere meaning the business owner or merchant's location independent. There is no warehouse, no sales location, no offices, not much employees and no hassles.

- There is little to absolutely no commitment to a physical space requirement which means the business owner can run their business by the beach, in their home, while flying on the plane. All you need is an internet connection and your laptop, iPad, tablet or any device you can access the internet with.

- You can sell just about anything over the internet and there's a dropship supplier for almost anything out there. Either sell only one product, or a mix of products - it is entirely up to you. Just find your niche and the right dropship supplier you need.

- You will have more time and resources to look into scaling your business. With traditional business models, the more you profit, the more work you have to put in and the more you need to invest in the resource section.

- Dropshipping also reduces losses on damaged goods. Shipment is directly from supplier to customer and because there are fewer shipment steps involved, the risk of the items being damaged is also reduced.

Cons of Dropshipping

Where there are pros, there are also cons even when it comes to dropshipping. Here are some of them:

- You must bear complete liability if anything goes wrong, even if it is the supplier's fault. The customer purchases the product from your site- the merchant's website. In the event, something happens or if the supplier doesn't keep their end of the bargain or messes up, it is still the merchant's fault. Your customers will contact you because you are the face of the brand. Therefore, it is extremely important to hire the right dropship supplier.

- You have lower control over the creative process. Your customers will have lesser satisfaction with your product because you will not be able to determine personalized packaging or the branding of the shipped products- this is dependent on the supplier.

- You have less control over how your product is presented during the fulfillment and delivery process as this is the supplier's job to ship the products to the customers. However, having the right supplier and establishing a good relationship with them will give you better control as some suppliers will go the extra mile in ensuring your creative process is delivered through the product. However, this may cost more.

- There may be more issues especially when it comes to shipping. Selling multiple products is a good idea as it can increase sales and make you profit, however, it can also pose a problem if the merchant has too many suppliers to deal with for each product they sell. Also, different suppliers will change different shipping costs as this would depend on where they are located and what kind of product you have.

- The competition in dropshipping retail is extremely high due to the attractiveness and the popularity of this business model. Unless the merchant caters to an extremely specific niche, the competition is detrimental.

- It is hard to keep track of the inventory from the supplier. Due to miscommunications due to cancellations and having backorders. However, with new software coming in and improved communication abilities, this matter can be solved. Of course, this software also comes with a price and may also increase your overhead costs.

How Viable and Profitable is Dropshipping?

Profit margins for dropshipping usually range from 15% to 45%. For consumer goods such as luxury items and durables, the profit margin can be up to 100%. When it comes to dropshipping, it entirely depends on the kind of niche you are in and then getting the right supplier. You do not want to enter a heavily saturated market.

One of the better ways to ensure higher margins is to source directly from the manufacturer and not the vendor/supplier. This cuts out the middleman. Once the business gains traction, it can become an effective money-making means that it only involves little input. To potential to earn up to one million dollars is real, although not for every dropshipping business.

Who is Dropshipping for?

If you are a first timer entering the online business, then dropshipping is a great business model, to begin with. It is low-risk and low-investment which is great for novices starting their own business. It does not involve much monetary gamble.

It is ideal for someone who is a current owner of a retail store and already has an inventory, but looking to reach newer, wider markets. This business model, however, does not give you amazing results from the get-go. Dropshipping margins are relatively lower so this might not bode well for a startup brand because these businesses do not have ultimate control where customer satisfaction, related to brand experience and branding is concerned.

Here Are the Types of Entrepreneurs Dropshipping Will Benefit:

- **The Validating Entrepreneur**

Dropshipping is a great way to test new products or even new startup products before an entrepreneur can begin heavily ingesting into the inventory required to sell. This makes it the perfect business model for entrepreneurs that require high levels of product validation before they begin investing heavily.

- **The Budget Entrepreneur**

Dropship qualifies as the least expensive business model for online selling because you do not need to purchase inventory upfront. Due to this, the dropshipping method sells effectively for entrepreneurs that are on a budget or are looking to keep startup costs low.

- **The First Time Entrepreneur**

Selling online is not as easy as it seems to be so for the first-time online entrepreneur, the dropshipping method works well. Understanding how to market the product online and drive and convert traffic takes time to figure out as well as optimize. Dropshipping allows online entrepreneurs to learn the ropes of online commerce, conversion and driving traffic before they begin investing thousands in an inventory.

- **The Multi-Variety Entrepreneur**

Dropshipping is an ideal model to use for retailers who want to sell a variety of products simple for the reason that you do not need to purchase inventory upfront.

Who Isn't Dropshipping for?

- **The Brand Centric Entrepreneur**

Building a brand around a product is difficult but the rewards are long-term and worthwhile. However, it is exponentially difficult to build a brand using the dropshipping retail method because there are plenty of other elements connected to the entire customer experience that the brand-centric entrepreneur will not be part of.

For instance, there will be times when a customer has made a purchase for a product. You, the merchant finds it's sold out with the dropship supplier. This is not only inconvenient for you as the merchant but also frustrating to the customer. It is even more frustrating to coordinate between dropshipper and customer to determine a solution. Since you are not shipping the product on your own, you also do not have control of the packaging which is an extension of the brand experience.

While some merchants are okay with that, asking yourself if this bothers you will help determine if dropshipping is for you. You also will not be able to create a relationship with shipping companies because you do not do the shipping. When something goes wrong in the shipping process, coordinating with the shipping companies can prove to be difficult. You need to coordinate with the shipping account representative, who is already busy, and this might take a few days to sort out.

- **The Margin Focused Entrepreneur**

One of the biggest problems with dropshipping is its thin margin lines. Gross margins for traditional dropshipping products is around 10 to 20%. After you pay off your credit card transaction fees, e-commerce fees, and other online services, you are looking at only a small percent of your margin left. While there are online entrepreneurs who earn big, up to a million dollars of revenue each year, their profit margins are around 40k to 50k once all these fees are deducted.

- **The Non-Creative Marketer**

With more manufacturers, chances are they're also dropshippers of their own products and they also have the same exact goals in sales which are about 30% coming from direct-to-consumer sales and this is usually from their own e-commerce site. This would mean that to sell their product, you are competing directly with your own supplier. This supplier has many other advantages such as higher margins than you on the same existing product.

Competing with them head-to-head is a waste of time and resource because most of the time, they win out all because they can afford to. You need to be creative and exploit other channels that they are not using to acquire the same target market and beat them. Relying on Google Adwords or Facebook Ads isn't going to cut it.

CHAPTER 2

Market Reserch And How To Find A Niche

While you don't need a business degree, investors, inventory or millions in capital as a traditional business, you definitely need some resources and the right approach. You need to have the right idea of what you are going to do. It's unwise to go into any business thinking you just want to make money fast. If you want to make money quickly, a traditional job will suffice where you get paid within your first month.

We've already established it's going to be completely online and most of, if not all, the heavy lifting is done for you. As well, you don't need a lot of money to start. What you'll need is a plan; a step-by-step blueprint of things to do now, today, and what's going to happen next. That's why this guide is so important.

It's easy to show you exactly how to find products, build your store and offer these products up for sale. It's going to look amazing once you do, but it would be an outright lie to tell you that you are going to be successful in taking this approach. It is the fun part yes, but one needs to fundamentally understand how they are going to bring a high level of value to their potential customers. That's choosing a 'good' niche and hence the 'right' products that will essentially fill a gap. Halfheartedly going about this is not going to yield the desired results. Worst, you are not going to sustain a long term business.

That said, don't worry right now about not having a niche, not knowing where to start and so forth because apart from having the resources and tools, which I will show you in subsequent chapters, you will know how to effectively deploy those tools and resources to gain maximum sales and profit.

Some people fail at dropshipping even with having all the tools, apps etc. simply because they are using the wrong approach.

Providing Value

It's the most important aspect of a successful dropshipping business. When thinking of value, there are at least three critical factors that should always remain at the forefront –

- What makes your company/business/product unique and different?
- What is it that your customers really want?
- Who are you going to work with to provide what they want?

Just because you're a dropshipper and reselling products, does not mean the products have to be cheaply made and don't do what they claim. If you have to rely on beautiful visuals and resorting to less than favourable tactics to get your product to sell or outsell your competition, then you're setting yourself up for failure.

Consumers aren't stupid. They're paying for something and they shouldn't get less than they deserve. Once you're able to see the benefits of a product, and you believe that it is something that will fill a gap in the market and the product isn't readily available and flooding the place everywhere you turn, you potentially have yourself a winning product that's going to provide value to the public. From there, you can build a reputation and it's going to mean more sales and profit for your business.

And it is actually doable. Some dropshippers will have all of these things in a product, but taking the wrong approach with no real strategy, is going to cause them to fail when trying to sell the product. I for one, have been able to sell products that were thought to be 'failures' because I was able to have a strategy in place, find and target the right audience and show them the benefits of and why they need it.

Think about any reputable and well-known business. They hardly, if ever, sell features. They sell benefits, experiences and they give value.

So in starting your business, whether choosing a niche, product and your marketing strategy, always think about value. Always think about who you're trying to help, how to put your customers first and make them feel like they're number one on your list of priorities and choosing products that are of high quality and high perceived value (more on this later).

The Right Niche Market

Niche Market: A small sector or portion of a market for a particular product.

I love any and everything to do with phones and electronics. I'm always reading and I'm always watching videos on my devices. That's what I'm interested in. Ah, there's my niche. I'm going to sell phone accessories, tablets and other electronics because I love them. My store is going to look awesome.

It's true, the store is going to look amazing but that's absolutely the wrong method of choosing a niche and you're going to be doomed to fail. It isn't just true for online businesses but also brick-and-mortar stores.

Why would anyone want to go into a market that is already saturated with tons of the same types of products? If you do so, in this example, try to sell phone cases, for one, it's very general, everyone uses it and there are hundreds, even thousands of online and offline stores that sell these to no one particular niche. It's difficult to pinpoint, and you're going to have issues trying to target the right audience, their interests and so forth.

Here is a better example. A portable folding fishing rod that's not bulky but sturdy and strong. It serves the outdoors market, which, of course, is very broad. However, you can narrow it down to people who like to fish. You can also further narrow this niche down to fly fishing, for example.

So your fishing rod is not a product that everyone uses, it has a specific audience, it may be unique to a lot of people in that area and there are so many benefits to it. Better, you're going to understand what they want (creating value) and how you're going to set out marketing the product to that audience. It is also going to give you an opportunity to discover and offer even more products in this niche that could be of tremendous usefulness to your core audience. It's going to be a lot less competitive and easier to be discovered than phone accessories.

With the niches that I have just listed above, which are only a tip of the iceberg, you can easily think of the vast array of those products flooding popular sites like Amazon and eBay.

Products Not To Sell

- Phone accessories (too competitive, it's going to be difficult to get noticed)
- Cosmetics (you don't want to go up against Maybelline and the like even though there are gadgets that sell insanely well once you find the right ones)
- Clothing (this is a very competitive market to get into, not to mention, hard to set up for first time dropshippers)
- Medical products (leave that to the experts, you don't need any problems)

There is hardly any real way of differentiating oneself and providing something truly unique in these spaces that will give value to your potential customers.

It isn't impossible however. But you will need to prepare for very stiff competition from other dropshipping stores that have been established for years. But if it is your goal and you have a strong foundation and have laid out a plan, there's no reason for you to turn your back on your goals.

With dropshipping, anyone can become a success story. An easier and more plausible approach however, is finding a niche that may not be that popular. As you can imagine, if a niche is not that popular, there may not be a lot of dropshipping stores selling products in that niche. There may be a high demand for certain products but limited suppliers, which is where you can step in, introduce products that you know the market will want and thus, make your mark in the dropshipping community. It's going to be less competition, you'll be able to differentiate yourself and you'll be the go-to for particular products because you've established yourself; you've been there longer.

Once you find this, always strive to stay ahead, always find ways of improving your store and looking for new customers.

The Right Product

You have not chosen a niche yet, but I hope you understand what goes into it. So, when you have chosen a niche, you'll need to select the right products.

Imagine you see an ad on your phone, laptop or other device for a pair of headphones. You get the product, it doesn't do what it says it will, it's cheaply made and it just doesn't look as attractive as it does in the video/photo that you saw.

What's going to happen is your ad is going to have a lot of negative reviews, more dislikes than likes and subsequently, you're going to have to deal with returns, customer service which I previously discussed, lower traffic and sales. That's because you didn't do enough homework on the product, you didn't properly 'feel out' the supplier and you paid the price.

Worst case scenario, you're going to spend time and/or money on advertising but you're not going to see any returns on investment. So trying to sell the most popular product isn't always the best way to go.

You need to be very selective and nit-picky about what you choose to sell. You need to once again, understand what your customer wants and need, and work with that to find products that will meet those wants and needs and yes, create value.

While choosing products that are already successful and popular is an excellent way to go (think of the fidget spinner where tons of dropshippers made thousands in sales) you need to consider how sustainable it's going to be.

Likewise, one should also be competent in analysing trends and use that to establish yourself in a certain niche and become profitable while sustaining profit. For example, it's a no-brainer that backpacks sell extremely well in particular months, but it's not going to be so throughout the year. However, if you find a product that is at the beginning of a trend and only began selling a few months ago, you have hit the jackpot because most likely, they're selling well.

I will discuss in further detail how to find products that has a high potential for profit. A great deal of your time will be spent on finding the right products for your customers. Remember, a lot of the public are not aware of many products that are available out there that is going to have a positive effect on their daily lives. It's up to you to find them. After all, it's what you're going to build your business around.

The Right Suppliers

There is a huge misconception that products that come from China are cheaply made, poorly designed and doesn't give satisfaction. This couldn't be further away from the truth. For one there are hundreds of first time as well as seasoned entrepreneurs who have and continue to use suppliers from China with much success.

The key to finding a good supplier will be to look at the numbers, the reviews about the quality of the products and so forth. As previously mentioned, suppliers are dropshippers as well who owe it to their customers to supply the best.

One of the most popular and successful dropshipping supplier is AliExpress who has gained the trust and respect of many dropshippers worldwide. It's not a fly-by-night organization and there are reputable dropshippers who source products directly from wholesalers.

The thing to be aware of is, you need to know how to choose your suppliers and be able to differentiate a good supplier from a bad one.

Once you have sourced a good supplier, you will then build a relationship with them which is going to make your life much easier and your customers happy.

If this seems daunting, have no fear. I will show you the methods that I and many other dropshippers use to obtain legitimate suppliers who you can come to rely on as your business grows and develops.

An Actionable Plan

It's worthwhile to have a plan or strategy of how you're going to approach your business in order to achieve your vision. Start by asking yourself first of all, what is the vision you have for your online ecommerce business.

To start with, it must be realistic and achievable. For example, where do you want to be in the next year? It could be that you want to earn a full time income and quit your job. You can even get more specific, you want to earn $10,000 or over $100,000 per month. More so, you may want to be able to make claims like, 'I made six figures in my third month as a dropshipper.'

Whatever your goals are, you need to take actionable steps to make it happen. You'll plan your time wisely, knowing how much effort you're going to put into it. How much money are you willing to spend on advertising and learning? Are you in it for the short term to 'see what happens?' Or are you serious and in it for the long term and you're going to make it work for you no matter what?

These are real questions that need answers. Make up your mind and then you can focus with a clear vision on the more minute details that are going to help you realize your goals for your business.

As well, what are you going to do if you're three months or six months in and you don't get the results you were expecting? Are you going to throw in the towel and say dropshipping doesn't work? And trust me, many people do this, which I don't mind because individuals who think this way were never in it from the start or for the right reasons, they don't really care about what they put out to the public and give dropshipping a bad rap.

Or if you 'fail' which I don't believe in, are you going to take the mistakes you make and use it as a learning experience to make things better? As Colin Powell said, there are no secrets to success. It is the result of preparation, hard work and learning from failure.

So now you have a clear idea of how you're going to start dropshipping and some of the most important things you need:-

- A good niche
- The right products
- Choosing the right suppliers
- A clear cut plan of what your goals are for your business.

Other Things You Need

PayPal, Stripe, Amazon Pay or any other type of financial institute is absolutely necessary for your Shopify store to collect payments from customers and also for you to receive funds. When you first set up your Shopify account, which is the best and easiest platform, in my opinion for first time dropshippers, you are given the different options to set up and verify your financial information.

Applying for any of these services are safe, secure and free. In my free Shopify 2019 Guide which you can download here, I show you exactly how to set up everything to get your store ready for your customers.

How Much Does Dropshipping Cost?

There is no standard amount for how much dropshipping costs. What may seem expensive or inexpensive to you can mean the direct opposite to someone else and vice versa. At this point in your business, you should focus on understanding how the process works, have a strategy of how you're going to get customers to your site and an idea of how you're going to scale and continue to make money with your store.

However, there are certain things you cannot do without when you're starting.

Shopify – With Shopify, you get a two week trial, so there's no cost there. After you have thoroughly gone through this guide; know your niche, know how to conduct product research, figured out your marketing strategy etc. then you can sign up for a Shopify account.

The reason is that you can then play around with the store, see how things work, add a few products, and make mistakes. After the two weeks, the basic price of a Shopify account is $29.

Shopify Apps – Even though you pay for your Shopify account, you're also going to need some apps on your store. Luckily, the most essential ones that you definitely cannot do without are free of charge. When you start to make money or even before you start to make money and you want to increase your chances of making sales, you can purchase some apps.

Most of the apps do come with a trial, and to actually pay the monthly fee for an app will cost you the price of selling a single product on your store so it's extremely reasonable.

Advertising – Social media, while it isn't the only way of advertising, has proven to be an excellent method for dropshippers, especially Facebook and Instagram ads which is my main strategy. There are literally more than 2 billion users on Facebook from all around the world at your fingertips. You have their demographics and psychographics and you can get them to click on your ad and go to your store.

CHAPTER 3

The Dropshipping Process

Should You Start Dropshipping?

Now that we know some of the pros and cons of dropshipping, it is worthwhile to ask yourself if dropshipping is really for you before actually delving into the detailed process of it. It's certainly not for everyone. But if you like the premise of being completely behind the scenes, researching, doing absolutely everything online (nobody has to personally know who you are, you don't have to talk to anyone, you're an introvert like me) you like trial and error, you like to get things up and running yourself and you stick to whatever plans you devise, then it's for you.

On the other hand, if you're looking to get rich quick or just sell anything to anyone in hopes of making a quick buck, then that screams scam and your business isn't going to go anywhere anytime.

You're going to be providing products to consumers and you need to do the work to ensure that those products are of high perceived quality, they do what they were advertised to do and that they're providing some sort of value to your customers. This is a mindset that you need to develop if you are not already thinking in terms of adding value.

Once again, don't be bogged down by fears of not having any experience in any of this because for the most part, anyone can do

23

dropshipping. Don't become stressed about not having enough time because you're not going to just quit your job and everything else and focus solely on this new venture.

Of course you can do this if you would like to, that would be excellent because you know exactly what you want and where you're heading. But dropshipping is a step by step process. You can do it to your leisure as a side hustle because maybe you don't want to quit your day job, or you just want some extra cash. Maybe you're a college student and you want to earn some more money.

Maybe you want to approach dropshipping aggressively and make it your full time ecommerce business. It's still flexible, you can scale it up/grow it rapidly and continue to grow and retain a customer base. The goal here will be to grow while keeping your costs low.

Once you have figured out the ins and outs of how to dropship and make it work in your favour, you're going to have so much time to yourself because you've mastered the art. That leaves you more time to do other business ventures to grow your wealth as many have done and are doing, or you can just spend more time doing whatever you want to do and love.

Anyone can do it. You don't need millions in capital and loans. You don't need to manufacture your own products without any real proof that you're going to make it in business.

The reason why thousands have been so successful in dropshipping is that it leaves a very clear footprint. It's like the fidget spinner (even though this was sort of a passing fad). There were ways to go about finding out if the fidget spinner was really something to start dropshipping. Through research, everything pointed to the fact that this product was a must sell product and as a result thousands of entrepreneurs made loads of money off of this.

There was no one supplier of this product. Likewise there are so many products out there selling like hot bread, and with the right tools, (this handy guide included) you can be one of the many businesses providing products and making enormous profits.

The Dropshipping Model

The dropshipping process is a simple and uncomplicated one.

Step #1 – The customer is directed to your store and purchases an item at the retail price of say, $300.

Step #2 – The merchant (you) receives this payment and information at their store from the customer then purchases the item at a wholesale price for $200, giving the supplier the customer's name and address.

Step #3 – The supplier ships the product directly to the customer's desired address. Your store makes a gross profit of $100.

But while simple at the forefront, it is important to know how this works at the backend. Why? Because you need to understand how to make your business flow smoothly and be as efficient and effective as possible. It is also crucial to know what your customer will experience during the buying process. A bad experience for the customer will no doubt end in fewer checkouts and thus low sales for your store. On the other hand, a good experience will make for quick sales and customer retention.

So first things first, let's see how the product moves from the supplier to the customer and everything in between.

The Manufacturer – Manufactures the products and then sells them in bulk to either suppliers or wholesalers. So they can sell to a supplier, for example in this case, someone from AliExpress. You, as the merchant, then buy from a supplier on AliExpress and the supplier ships the product to your customer.

You can also purchase directly from the manufacturer at a significantly cheaper price than a supplier.

Suppliers and Wholesalers – Sell products they have sourced to retailers. The benefit to purchasing from a supplier is that it's easier and sometimes they specialize in a specific niche so once you find your niche and a good supplier, you make your process simple by building a relationship with your supplier. The downfall, not a bad one, is that the supplier will charge you more than a manufacturer. But, you also charge your customers more than you paid your supplier.

Retailers – In this case you as the merchant sells the products that you sourced from your supplier to the public where the supplier will dropship to the customer. To do all of this, you open an online ecommerce store and stock it with non-physical products, meaning images, descriptions and prices.

The above image is an example of a highly successful dropshipping store that rakes in 6 and 7 figures per month. Note that it has a very simple layout and offers basically one product. It is very successful because the product is in high demand, it solves a problem and isn't readily available in stores.

You don't need any experience and you don't need to know a single line of code. Everything is point-and-click, drag and drop. The free guide is more practical in that you already know how the business works, what you need to do and what you're going to sell. So it would just be to get the ball rolling.

Note: Download the free step-by-step guide on building your Shopify store. You will learn how to customize your storefront to give it a professional look and feel, add products from trusted suppliers and much more. Click here to download.

The main focus of this guide is to show you how to become the retailer who purchases from suppliers and then sells to the public. I can't stress enough how important this is. Some first time dropshippers have a very basic and unfortunately poor understanding of what it takes to run a business like this, therefore they run into obstacles they weren't aware of and walk away believing that the model does not work rather than realizing that they have done things the wrong way and didn't take the time to learn and understand how it works.

The Process as the Customer Sees It

I'm assuming that you have made multiple purchases online in the past whether it's from eBay, Amazon, Newegg or wherever. Think about what your experiences have been like. Was it simple? Was it straight to the point? Did you encounter any problems that you just couldn't get answers to or couldn't find a customer service rep when you really needed one?

All consumers at some point in time, may encounter an issue while others may not. Your job as the retailer is to minimize problems and potential issues by making the buying process as simple and painless as possible because this is what the customer wants.

For example, you want to make the experience as follows:

- A customer comes to your online storefront and orders an item. They get instant email notification of their purchase and the cost.
- Depending on your shipping time, the customer then receives either a few hours or days after purchase, that their item has been shipped to the desired address. They also receive information on how they can track their package. (There are apps for all of this which I will cover in the free Shopify guide here.)
- The customer receives their item in the allotted time.

So this has been a painless and convenient process for the customer. What it means for your business is a good reputation, trust building, and the customer does not have to interact with customer service which you don't want to have to deal with especially at the beginning.

As well, the customer has no clue that you're the middleman or that any other parties are involved. They bought the product from your store that has your name/name of your business on it.

The Process as the Retailer Sees It

- So you notice that you have an order for one of your products. You're happy, it's just the beginning and you're motivated to say the least.

Your store, Cell Luxury, will receive the same email confirmation along with the customer's payment.

- Cell Luxury then sends an order to the supplier who then processes your order. You, Cell Luxury, will be charged for making that purchase. And say the entire amount, including shipping of the case will cost a total of $12.46. This means that your profit will be $7.49. Not bad at all.
- So you ordered the cell phone case and the supplier packages your order. Well, the supplier is going to address the package from Cell Luxury and Cell Luxury's name will be displayed on the invoice and packaging slip. The supplier will then send all this information to you.
- Then last, but not least, this information will be automatically sent to your customer through whatever app you decided to

download to do this for you. The customer receives their cell phone case, they're happy, you're happy.

So you do two things in the dropshipping process. You make the orders from the supplier when you actually get a sale, and provide them with the shipping information of the customer.

That's dropshipping in a nutshell.

Note: When starting dropshipping as a small business/sole proprietorship, it is common to use one's own funds for example a credit card. Since platforms, example Shopify, doesn't pay immediately, you can use your own card to fulfil orders, meaning, buy the items from your credit card as orders come in. Therefore, it is a good idea to forecast how much sales you plan to make and have a budget to start with. Or you can wait a couple days to have funds from sales transferred to your account.

CHAPTER 4

Setting Up Your Dropshipping Business

How to find a niche

When you are starting your business, there are multiple factors you need to keep in mind and it is up to you to create a balance and sync all these variables with one another. However, as it all begins with you settling for a niche, it is mandatory for you to invest time and effort into picking the best one for your business. When doing so, you should consider going for something that has sufficient demand and which you can be confident about selling a good minimum number per day. This is a good indicator for you to understand whether this niche will be a good long-term investment or not. The niche should not suffer from changes in season or climate. You should lookout for a product that is not in an overly competitive market. On the other hand, you should think more strategically and look for keywords that are not frequently used by your competitors. For a single product, you and your competitors may use the same search words; if you have different words, it can help you gain a competitive advantage over the others from the very beginning. You should remember to consider the size and dimensions of your product; you should opt for something small and light as it will be easier for your suppliers to ship out to your customers. In the end, running a business and putting that much effort in should help you make a profit and you should choose a product that will complement this. According to a lot of dropshippers, when you start out, you should set a target to have around ten sales a day, regardless of your product type. However, depending upon your niche, you can set the percentage of profit you want to make per sale.

How to find suppliers

After you have selected a niche, you should look out for suppliers according to your niche. You can start by looking for suppliers who are near you, however, you should be open to suppliers based in another state or even country. In most cases, you will notice that suppliers are based internationally and that you have to dropship from there. Try to keep in mind that the further your suppliers are, the higher the possibility of having delays in shipment times. Having said this, you should prioritize quality over quantity and go for the ones with more experience in providing products in your niche. You need to do extensive research to find the suppliers as you will notice that suppliers who have been in business since the beginning of dropshipping do not focus much on customer service and communication. They tend to have a very outdated website with basic information on it. You should be ready to expect hurdles like this and call or email these suppliers to talk about their pricing and policies regarding returns and refunds in detail. Besides, there are various online tools available that help you locate suppliers according to your niche; you can also opt for more personalized service.

How to choose a product

Choosing a product among so many can be a tough task and under no circumstances should it be done in a rush. If needed, you should take your time and have discussions with people face to face to gain perspective. There are a couple of factors that work together to help you choose a product for your store. Firstly, try to get help from other online communities and online stores that are in the same niche to help you brainstorm efficiently. Doing this will give you some ideas and allow you to compare these product ideas to your target price range. Doing this will help you narrow the list down even further. You can use online tools such as Google Trends to make comparisons on a local and global scale for these chosen products. You can filter out the results and see how well these products may work out for your dropshipping store. You should compare data obtained for the sales and profit margins of these products to help you cut down more from the list until you are left with the best one to match your business goals.

How to create your business

The previously mentioned processes of finding a niche, a supplier, and a product were just a few of the important steps of starting a business. However, before even thinking of getting involved with these stakeholders, you should be able to develop a dropshipping business concept that is marketable. This will help you draft out your long-term and short-term plans and help you assess your progress as you move along the way. In the meantime, you need to get registered with your government if you want to become a fully functioning enterprise and make everything legal and official. You need to have a dropshipping website that is the best representation of your niche and your product line. You should invest in this and hire professionals to work on building this store for you if needed. When your website is ready, you should be ready to add products to it. You should be careful when doing so and do prior research before settling on a niche. You should have direct communication with your supplier to check the availability of items before adding them to your store. Lastly, after you have a fully functioning website that has all the products you want to sell, you need to allocate some resources to promote your store and manage the day to day activities.

How to get permits and licenses

After you are done setting up your business, you need to deal with the legal aspects and think about getting permits and licenses. For starting a business in the US, the very first step would be to register your dropshipping business with your state where you should expect to pay around $150 to $300, depending upon the type of products your business is targeting to sell. This makes you eligible to obtain an EIN (Employer Identification Number) from the IRS (Internal Revenue Service) - this does not require you to pay a fee and you should be able to receive the EIN smoothly. Afterward, you need to make a requisition in your respective state for a sales tax ID. This is also free unless your state is an exception where you need to pay a sales tax. You need to open an account to show that you are in an established relationship with a dropshipper, which should also be free of cost. Lastly, it is highly recommended that you get your website made beforehand as things will be much easier to verify if any legal issues occur. There are exceptions to this process, especially regarding total cost; however, for a dropshipping business, $400 is more than enough to get started.

How to choose a sales platform

There are various platforms that you should consider when choosing one for your dropshipping store. Firstly, if your main focus is to earn money within the shortest possible time frame, then it would be best for you to dropship on your own website. This will allow you to stand out from the crowd and have control over the operations. You will not be exempted to pay fees as you will have to pay them when you are dealing with Amazon and eBay. You can be sure to get more exposure for your products when you are engaged with Amazon and eBay, as customers will trust them more. You can even get access to Fulfillment by Amazon FBA (if you use Amazon). On eBay, the website is extensive yet easy to navigate for the customers, but the auction-style may not be fully suited to the dropshipping industry. On the other hand, it will take longer for you to gain a large customer base, so it might be better to go with Amazon and eBay. It totally depends on where you want to see your business in the long run and how the sales platform will bring more value to your customers.

How to create a payment system

Today, there are multiple methods of accepting and receiving payments and it is recommended for you to be aware of all of them. You should offer ease and convenience regarding payment methods for your customers and ensure that they feel safe with the choices you have given them. PayPal is the best choice in most cases and it is accessible anywhere. It is wise to use the most common platforms people use but you should look into the demographics of your target customers and see what would be the most convenient for them. If you need to accept bank transfers, you should make arrangements for that beforehand. You should also research what the most popular and respectable method of payment is in the region you are expecting to sell in.

How to set up a customer service system

Regardless of your niche or industry, customer service should always be a priority. The customers remember their experience, so if they had a positive experience, they will definitely share this among their peers, who in turn contribute to bringing new customers to your store. However, negative experiences have the potential to completely ruin your venture. You need to be careful when assigning any of your employees to handle the customer service department. You can set up a helpline or give the official email address of the company where they can make product requests. Moreover, you can offer live chat sessions with them at set hours with regular phone call facilities on toll-free numbers. You can think of email marketing in this case and can send forms out to your customers after they have made a purchase to get their feedback. Try to keep the form in the form of short answers or multiple-choice answers; filling out the form should be hassle-free and efficient for them.

How to create a list of offerings

Your niche is what you design your entire business around. Within that niche, try to find out what products have a higher probability to make sales. These are the ones you should target and try to figure out whether these products will be trendy in the near future or not. You can also try to analyze the proportion of profit you can make per sale among these products within your niche to make thorough comparisons. You may need to conduct surveys or study surveys conducted before to understand the nature of the market and to be aware of what is in demand. Considering all of this, you can start creating a list that will be posted on your website for customers to keep track of what is available and what is not. You can divide them into categories, in terms of price range or season for example. The information you acquired has to be relevant to your niche and needs to be updated at regular intervals. It is better to use online tools when you are starting out as the process would make it easier to keep track of additions throughout.

How to purchase the product from the supplier whenever you make a sale

When you have received an order from a customer, you are now sure that there is a specific buyer for this item and now you can go ahead and buy it from your supplier. You should not stock up on inventory because it gives you uncertainty and prevents you from investing in other sectors of your business. Dropshipping does not encourage you to buy products in bulk. The trends may change and customers may be more inclined to buy whatever is trendy. If you make bulk purchases, you cannot invest in other products as your money is already stuck with those orders. You should confirm with your supplier before confirming with your customer about the availability of the product. You should focus on using online management software that lets you keep tabs on the number of purchases made along with their prices and estimated dates of delivery. You can also keep a manual list and send your supplier a hard copy of the invoice.

How to find ways to market your business

Marketing your business is essential to be able to compete or even initially just survive in the industry. Due to not having any restrictions to enter the market, the dropshipping industry tends to become more and more competitive every day. Thus, you should do everything within your reach to make the most of the online platforms available to you.

Answering Questions

You can drive traffic to your store by paying more attention to your customers. You can assign an employee as a social media manager or you, yourself can be in charge of this. Platforms like Reddit and Quora are a great way to gain exposure where you can link back to a blog post you have written on your store or provide a link to your website each time you respond with an answer or leave a comment. This will attract new customers and also help you connect with the ones who commented on the post initially. For Reddit, you will find divisions or sections known as subreddits for niches that your store is related to. You can be part of multiple subreddits as long as they are related to your niche and product line. You can even get ideas from others who are adopting this tactic. On the other hand, for Quora, the system is more straightforward. As it is a question-answer based site, you can pose questions or answer any question that is related to your niche, but you should remember to link it back to your blog or online store. Lastly, there are separate forums available on various kinds of niches where you can apply the same tactics. Overall, your focus should be to add value through these platforms in the long run.

Affiliate program for your dropshipping store

This is a very unique strategy for when you have gained a solid customer fan base. For total newcomers, making this work will be a challenge since the very concept of affiliate marketing depends on whether you have sufficient traffic to your store for this tactic to work. The affiliate program motivates people to market the products in your dropshipping store. The higher the number of people involved in doing affiliate marketing for your dropshipping, the higher the probability of your sales increasing. These people get a certain share in percentage from the sales they are bringing in. The total revenue that you earn through the affiliate program is comparatively higher than that of other strategies. Here, you are paying the people not from your business funds but from the revenue they are bringing in for you. This helps you to thrive and acquire more customers.

Email marketing

This strategy is to increase your customer retention rate. The customers who have made purchases from you before can be significant, as well as new customers that you seek to sustain, both in the long run and in the short term. If they do not come back, it implies that your competitor may have been able to add that customer to their customer base; this becomes a setback for you. Initially, you can see it happening with one or two customers, but over time it can become a trend and it will be too late for you to recover. Hence, email marketing is suggested in order to keep them coming back. You can do it through sending various offers during holidays, or encouraging them to subscribe to your blog; this depends on your target demographic so you need to learn how to grab their attention.

CHAPTER 5

Find The Right Products

The Basics of Selling Products Online

Every business needs a good marketing strategy to work. When you start out, virtually no one knows about your business, the products you offer, and your terms. Before customers can start buying from you, it is important that you start reaching out to them, making them aware of your business. In this chapter, we shall look at the different avenues where you can reach out to people willing to pay for your products and the strategies that you can use to do so.

When deciding to start advertising on either of these channels, you should consider the money you intend to use in your marketing efforts. You can then evaluate each advertisement medium and allocate a portion of your total budget based on its effectiveness. Starting out, a daily budget of about $10 spread between Facebook, Pinterest, is recommended. Henceforth, you can increase the budget on each platform based on the results of each post.

If you are a novice in the dropshipping business, you could end up wasting a lot of time trying to figure out the ins and outs of running the business. To enable you to hit the ground running and to get ahead of the learning curve, let's discuss how you should operate your business once it's fully set up.

41

First, you have to understand that things are going to get mixed up at some point—that is the nature of the dropshipping business. The fact that most logistical functions are handled by third parties (manufacturers, wholesalers, and suppliers) means that there are lots of things that are out of your control, and so you should be mentally prepared to deal with mistakes and screw-ups.

Your suppliers will occasionally mess up your customers' orders, and sometimes, they may even run out of stock. When this happens, you may feel frustrated, and you may be tempted to give in or even to switch to a different business model. We can't lie to you and say that there won't be any challenges, but we can guarantee you that you will be able to handle most challenges if you are adequately prepared, and if you have taken the time to establish rules and protocols for all types of challenging scenarios.

One thing you need to remember is that the dropshipping model is already complicated by its very nature, so you should try as much as possible to keep things simple on your end. Try to find simple solutions to any problems that arise, rather than wasting time and resources trying to figure out the perfect solution for your problems. Things move fast in this business, and if you focus too much attention on singular events, you are going to get overwhelmed. Have a simple structure for your business, and make sure that all your operations move along smoothly.

Since mistakes are bound to happen, you shouldn't spin your wheels too much when they actually do occur. Even the best suppliers will occasionally mess up an order, and the customer will end up getting disappointed by the package he receives. Whatever the error, don't waste time passing around blame.

When addressing a customer's complaint, own up to the mistake and apologize, then take quick measures to make it up to him by seeing to it that your supplier fixes the issue. Think of every mistake as an opportunity to learn and grow.

Most professional suppliers will own up to mistakes that are genuinely theirs, so you don't have to be too confrontational when you report your customers' complaints to them. It's important to maintain a good rapport with your suppliers throughout because your success as a drop-shipper depends on it. However, if a supplier makes a habit out of messing up your orders, it may be wise to conclude your association with that supplier, because he may drag you down the path of failure.

Even though drop-shippers don't personally handle inventory, one of the biggest challenges that you will have to deal with as a drop-shipper will be the management and coordination of inventory, given the fact that you will most likely be working with multiple suppliers (we've already discussed why it's important to build redundancy into your supply system by having backup suppliers for each product in case there is a problem with your primary supplier). Managing and monitoring inventory is quite complicated, but as you gain more experience, you will become much better at it.

Even if you have a supplier and a backup supplier for a given product, you should keep a list of every other supplier who stocks the products that you are selling so that you can monitor things like price changes or the introduction of new models of the product to the market. If you don't keep tabs on all suppliers in the market, you could miss major market changes that could either render your prices unsustainable or make your products less viable. For instance, if you sell fashion accessories, your suppliers may be late to introduce new trendy items, and you would be stuck selling outdated items while your competitors cash in on the new trend.

If multiple suppliers are operating in the same niche, they may not all stock the same exact products, but chances are they all have the best-selling items in their catalogs. Always go with the supplier who offers you the best deal and don't be too hung up on loyalty—your primary aim is to increase your profit margin and make more money.

You should also exercise a lot of wisdom when selecting the products that you want to carry in your store. Try to select products that are readily available in multiple stores so that you can always have options when you have lots of order to fulfill. If you pick a product that is only available from one supplier, you run a much bigger risk of failing to fulfill an order if your supplier runs out of stock because there are no other sources of that product.

Find High Demand Products

Picking Products That Are Popular

The first and possibly most obvious thing that you want to do for your business is picking products that are going to be popular amongst your niche audience. You want to make sure that you are going to be selling things that people actually want to be buying. Picking products that are popular will help you with creating a strong shop that is filled with interesting, attractive items that excite people and encourage them to pay attention to your shop.

You can identify which products are the most popular in your industry by going to platforms like Amazon and Etsy and searching for keywords that are relevant to your industry. Doing this will take you to the category relevant to your business, which will then show you the most popular items that people are purchasing. Depending on what platform you are on, you may need to adjust your sorting settings to say "Top-Rated" or "Best Selling." Choosing these search parameters will ensure that everything that is being shown to you is what people are actually purchasing on a regular basis, and not just what has been posted or sponsored by the people selling said product.

After you have searched on these platforms, you will get a general idea for what types of products are selling the best. Then, you can use platforms like Google Trends to do research on said product so that you can begin to see whether or not it is actually popular enough for you to stock in your shop. Ideally, the product should have a strong uptrend behind it, but it should not be at its peak trend. Any product that is in peak search numbers, based on the parameters given to you by platforms like Google Trend, is likely to be too competitive for you to make sales in. You want products that are going to be popular, but not oversaturated to avoid having to attempt to compete with far too many brands that are already out there selling products to your target audience.

To help get your shop started, you want to identify about 30-50 popular products that you could sell in your shop. This may sound like a lot, but it will be narrowed down through the following steps to about 15-30 new products that you can stock your shop with. This is plenty for a new dropshipping company to start with and leaves you with space for growth over time, so avoid going much higher than this number.

Pricing Your Products Effectively

As you go through the most popular products that you could potentially stock your shop with, you want to make sure that you also jot down how much money you could charge per item. This is going to be helpful with determining what your profit margins would be later on, while also giving you an idea of how you can use your price points to position yourself in the market.

When it comes to price points, you want to look around and see what the exact same products are going for in other shops. As you do, seek to identify the lowest price point in the market and the highest price point in the market. Then, try to identify the most popular price point, which will be the price point that has made the most sales. You might expect that the lowest price point would be the one making the most sales, but the truth is most consumers consider products that are priced too cheaply to be cheaply made. In many instances, dropshippers that are pricing at the lowest possible prices are seen as companies that work with low-quality suppliers, resulting in people being skeptical about ordering through their business at all. For your business, you want to price around the mid-point or slightly lower or higher depending on what you want your positioning to be. If you want to be

Dropshipping

considered inexpensive or affordable, you want to make sure that you are using the lower end of the midway point. If you want people to perceive you as being a more high-end boutique shop, price slightly higher. This way, you leverage your pricing as your positioning as well by using it to help influence how others perceive your business.

Ensuring that the profit Margins Are Big Enough

After you have identified the ideal products that you can stock your shop with, you want to make sure that your profit margins are big enough. Your profit margins are calculated based on the amount of money that it is going to cost for you to stock items in your shop, versus the price that you are going to sell your products at. To calculate your true price points, you need to factor in the cost of running your business combined with the cost of the product itself when you order it from your supplier.

Ideally, the products you sell should have at least a 30% or larger profit margin as this will ensure that you produce enough money to pay for listing and selling the product, while also making a profit on top of that. Anything too far below 30% is going to likely prove unworthy of selling as it will not earn you enough to really run your business. Unless you are making a decent profit margin that covers the cost of selling that product and you are selling high volumes of it, there is no point stocking anything with a lower margin.

It is important to understand that the more popular your products are in the industry, the less your profit margin is going to be because you have such a large competition amongst you. This is why it pays to pick products that are popular but not overly saturated, as it helps ensure that you are getting the right profits and attention on your products for you to succeed with.

Analyze your Competitors

Use Tools Available Online

There are site explorers like SEMrush which help you in checking the domain authority and rank of a website using a URL. You can use them to get a clear picture of the amount of traffic that is driven to their website from keywords as well as from other links. You can also personally observe their sites and get an insight into the way they function.

Order Items from Your Competitors

There may be a difference between what appears online and the real things that take place. So, it is a good idea to order something from your competitor's website. This will enable you to become familiar with the peculiarities that make them a unique enterprise, or the negative aspects of the brand experience provided by them. You may even get some tips to improve your own enterprise.

However, there is no need to copy their entire process of working. Just observe if there are any flaws which you can avoid and improve your customer's experience.

Analyze Your Competitor's Social Network

The social channels of your competitor are an important means of getting direct feedback from the customers about his business. They also provide a basis on which you can analyze your rival's marketing strategy. You can check how well their brand is performing and what are the flaws. You can work on these to enhance your brand.

CHAPTER 6

Working With Suppliers

Finding a reliable supplier is one of the biggest stumbling blocks for every dropshipper. That is why this is one of the most important things that you need to decide on.

You may be a great marketer but if your supplier screws up then you end up trying to fix things. And a lot of times the causes of these troubles were outside your control in the first place.

You should take every precaution to find the right suppliers. There are several strategies that you can use. With some practice you will learn to spot a reliable wholesaler and avoid the bad ones.

The Makings of a Good Dropshipping Supplier

The following are the characteristics of a great dropshipping supplier:

1. The Absence of Huge Per-Order Fees

Wholesalers and suppliers will usually charge what is called a per-order fee. This is a fee that covers for the time and resources necessary to get your order packed and shipped to your customers.

Some suppliers take advantage of this and will charge a rather high fee. So, how much of a fee are we looking at? It usually ranges anywhere from $2 to $10 (and sometimes higher).

You should factor that when you select products since this fee will be added to the actual product price that you need to display on your ecommerce site.

Sometimes the fee can get too high and you end up reducing your profit margin. Remember that $10 might not sound much but if your competitor can lower their prices by $5 because their supplier charges them less then you can bet customers will choose to do business with them instead.

2. Quality Products

Here's a rule of thumb. If you provide quality products then you should expect lower product return orders from your customers. It also translates to the following:

- Better product reviews, which in turn boosts sales
- Fewer returns
- More organic and word of mouth referrals
- Higher rate of customer satisfaction

Are there any downsides to finding a supplier that can provide you with quality products? Well, I can think of only one—possibly lower margins.

That means you can't jack up the prices of your products a lot higher. However, even if you don't make a huge amount of profit per product sale, you will end up getting more profit from volume sales.

The more satisfied customers you have the more potential repeat orders you will get. That can also translate to more profits from referrals and the increased number of customers.

Yes, you may get low margin per sale. But that is a lot better than getting high margin sales but low quality products. It will not benefit you in the long run.

3. They Give You Access to Big Name Brands

Earlier it was mentioned that you should avoid big brand products. Yes it is true. But that is a rule for beginners—hope that clarifies things. After your dropshipping business becomes a big hit you might want to look into selling big brand products.

Brand name products also represent better quality products. A good and reliable wholesaler is one that can supply you these products. If big name brands trust them then you can trust them as well.

4. Helpful Representatives and Years of Experience

Of course it goes without saying that you should look for a supplier who has been doing it for a while. Their years of experience sending products to customers will be a big thing to lean on especially when untoward incidents happen.

That means if there is a botched delivery (e.g. damaged goods upon delivery, wrong delivery, missing items etc.) then you can coordinate with the supplier to amend the situation.

No one is perfect—we should all know that by now. And even the best suppliers and wholesalers who employ the highest standards will make mistakes from time to time.

Remember that these businesses manage hundreds if not thousands of orders every single day. Mistakes and blunders will happen every time that happens. You can chalk it up to Murphy's Law I guess.

If there is one thing that can make up for that is rep from the supplier that you can talk to that can answer all your questions. Of course, you can't expect them to know all the answers but the really good reps would be more than willing to find out what happened to an order and get back to you.

They will know how to handle any issues that come along. They will also be able to answer any questions that you might have. And if they don't have an answer at that moment they will go out of their way to find out and give you an update.

5. Fast Shipping

Delays will always make customers unhappy—and obviously you don't want that in your dropshipping business. If your supplier can't deliver the goods in 24 hours then they are not good for this kind of enterprise.

But you can give them a 24 to 48 hour window to get the goods delivered. However, do take note that a48 hour delivery window is pushing it.

Dropshipping is a very competitive business. There is no room here for delayed shipments. If your ecommerce store is known for delays then your competition will eat you alive.

However, if you do find a wholesaler or a supplier that delivers things on time every time, then you have just found a goldmine. You already have a competitive edge.

Customers will like that a lot. Now, you can test your supplier by creating a test order. Order something yourself and have it shipped to you.

That way you get first-hand experience at how fast the supplier gets the order delivered. And you also get to see the quality of their service. You can do this to test two different suppliers or wholesalers. The one that can get things done in record time should be the winner.

6. Technologically Invested

You're going to be running a store that will be cloud based. That means you need to partner with someone or another business that is also just as committed to technology as you are.

Your supplier should be one that also takes advantage of the latest technologies. That means that both of you should be on the same page when it comes to automation, scalability, and of course efficiency.

Dropshipping

This will be increasingly important as your dropshipping enterprise grows and of course along with that comes an increase in the number of orders. The more customers you serve the more difficult it will be to manage these orders if your supplier is still doing things manually or on paper.

Remember that you may not be the only dropshipper that your wholesaler is serving. If it is a good wholesaler then chances are that other dropshippers will also take advantage of their services as well.

Now, how do you know if a wholesaler or supplier is also invested in today's technology? They should have at least the following:

- They have automated order placement and order cancellation.
- There are also options to place and also cancel orders via email
- Their product listings are updated as fast as their inventory listings
- The products on their website have updated and detailed information.

Note that not all suppliers will have all of that information readily available on their website. But if there is a number that you can call and the support staff can answer all of your questions then you might be looking at a good provider—their tech needs to catch up but they'll get there one day.

Note also that you shouldn't also judge a supplier based on how good looking their site is – if there is a secondary method to get you the info that you need then they're good to go.

7. Dedicated Support Reps

The sales rep that answered your call or product inquiry shouldn't be the same person you talk to if something goes wrong with your order. In fact the really good supplier can assign a representative to you to help monitor your situation until it is resolved.

8. Order by Email or by Phone

This is a small thing but this can actually go a long way. There should be alternative ways to place an order. What if the supplier's website experiences a downtime and you have lots of orders?

If a supplier can accommodate other methods of placing and managing orders then you immediately solve a problem right there. At least you know that this wholesaler or supplier can manage and fulfill orders during difficult situations.

How to Find a Great Supplier

Again, the goal is to find a supplier or wholesaler that is reliable and also legit for that matter. One of the simplest ways to find a good dropshipping supplier is to do a Google search.

The easiest way to find a supplier is of course through Google. You just need to open your browser and use the following search term:

<name of product> + dropshipping supplier + <country or location>

Here's a sample search term I used:

socks dropshipping suppliers Australia

And that pulled up over a million results. I didn't know it would pull up that many search results. But if you look closely the SERPs provided by our favorite search engine really didn't give me purely a list of supplier websites.

Some of the websites listed on the first few pages weren't even in Australia. Some were lists of wholesale sock manufacturers in China, UK, and the US. I guess these manufacturers also ship to Australia, which is why they're on the top of the list—not sure though.

Of course with that many on the list it will be like looking for a needle in a haystack, right?

Attend a Trade Show

Trade shows don't happen a lot but when one does you should make the effort to attend it. This way you can find out who the manufacturer is. You can even come up to a rep or the manager and ask for information yourself.

Find the suppliers and manufacturers that provide the products you are interested in. You can ask for their contact info and introduce yourself as retailer interested in their products. You can then ask them questions like payment terms, warranties, and others (more about that later).

Order from the Competition

This is a good trick that you can do if you know that a competing ecommerce store is actually dropshipping their products. Here's how you do it.

Make a small order of the product that you are interested in. When the product arrives check out the return address. Look it up on Google and see which business is on that property.

Sometimes it works and sometimes it doesn't. This at least gives you an idea who the original shipper is—which may likely be the wholesaler or the manufacturer. The next step is to get that company's contact information.

Look for Dropshipping Supplier Directories

So, doing a Google search can give you an idea but you will have to fine tune your search. You need to use something better. So, what is better than organic Google searches?

You need to search for supplier directory sites. Using supplier directory sites is a kind of shortcut since the people behind these sites have done the background research for you. Here are some of the benefits that you can get from using them:

- Faster research – you can quickly find out the product offerings of each supplier. Some suppliers are listed by product type. Their contact information is already given.

- Easier searches – you can easily filter out the search by different category. You can filter the results by product, price range, and other specs that you need.
- Lowers your risk – the list provider has done the grunt work and has taken out the scammers.

List of Popular Suppliers

We have a list of the most popular suppliers below. The information about each of these suppliers can help you decide which one to choose for each particular product. Note that there are pros and cons to using their services.

Since they are popular and highly rated then you can be sure that they offer the best delivery and also have some of the best products. However, since they are popular you should know that you're not the only dropshipper that will take advantage of their services.

That means that there will be times when these guys will be overloaded with orders that they might have trouble keeping up. Some of the businesses in the list below aren't necessarily wholesalers. Some of them are online directories that will point you to actual suppliers.

1. **AliExpress**

This is one of the most popular dropshipping platforms and also a wholesaler. They also help connect dropshippers like you to actual suppliers. Take note that a lot of their suppliers are from China.

However, take note that their suppliers are a mix—some are good and some are not so good. If you want to make sure then run a test order.

The good news is that they have suppliers from more than 40 niche categories—which is a lot. You can find pretty much everything from apparel to electronics. The other good news about them is that they have free sign up.

2. Doba

This is actually a marketplace where manufacturers and suppliers are listed. You can search for suppliers and manufacturers by product or industry. They have done the research for you so can find good suppliers for your selected product. The downside is that their service comes with a monthly fee of $29 (minimum).

3. Worldwide Brands

This is a massive directory of bulk distributors and wholesalers. Their list of suppliers covers pretty much every niche you can think of. The best part is that they make sure that each company on their list is reliable and reputable. The downside is that there is a huge one-time fee to sign up with them amounting to $249.

4. Dropship Direct

This is a general supplier and they offer more than 100,000 products on their list. The products are all shipped from their warehouses. Other than a huge product list and an expansive warehouse system they also offer you data on the different products such as the number of orders, cancel rates, etc. on each product.

They provide you with a lot of metrics that will help you decide if a product will sell well or not. On top of that, they have free sign up.

5. Mega Goods

If you're interested in selling electronics then this is the supplier that you might want to check out. Their products include Bluetooth devices, TVs, kitchen appliances, cameras, clocks, and others. They charge a service fee of $14.99 per month.

6. National Dropshippers

This is a wholesaler that has more than 250,000 products in their warehouses. Since they are a huge warehousing company they can offer products at 50% MSRP, which can potentially increase your margin per sale.

The downside is that they have monthly service fee of $19.99 and they charge you $2.49 for each order they serve.

7. Dropshipper.com

This is a dropshipper platform and they connect you to more than 890 suppliers. They have a massive product listing of almost 2 million types of products. They have everything from electronics to beauty products.

They charge a one-time fee of $99. It's either that or you pay a monthly fee of $69.

8. Inventory Source

This is actually a dropshipping network that can connect you to more than 150 suppliers. They also connect you to dropshipping platforms such as Amazon, eBay, Shopify, BigCommerce, and the like. Their service plans start at $50 a month.

9. Sunrise Wholesale

This is actually a wholesaler that offers more than 15,000 types of products. Their product categories include garden decorations, jewelry, sports and fitness, home decors, and lots more. They also connect you to dropshipping platforms like Amazon, eBay, and Shopify among others. They require a membership fee of $39.95 per month or $99 each year.

10. Wholesale Central

This is another wholesaler or supplier directory. And the good news is that it is free to access. You can search their directly using different filters. You can also search by product niche such as pet supplies, candles, books, and eye wear among others.

CHAPTER 7

How To Dropship With Shopify

S hopify is by far the best online tool for drop-shippers who don't have the technical expertise to create their own shops. It makes it possible for anyone to sign up and start his own online store in just a few minutes. It's great for people who want to start a dropshipping business but lack the technical know-how or the resources to build their own e-commerce websites from scratch. If you want a hassle-free experience as you start your first store, you should seriously consider using Shopify. The service offers free trial periods for beginners who want to test the waters before making a financial commitment. Here is a step by step guide to help you start your first Shopify dropshipping store.

Choose a Name for Your Dropshipping Store

When creating a Shopify store, your first task will be to select a name for your dropshipping business. You want to make sure that the name you select is simple, creative, and memorable. If you already have a niche in mind, you could try to find a name that is related to that niche so that people can have an easy time figuring out what you are selling. There are some online business name generators that you could use to come up with a list of possible names before you narrow it down to one.

When you find a few possible names that you may want to use, you must check to see if they are available. Google each of your shortlisted business names to see if they are already in use. If you use obvious sounding names such as "American Watches," chances are someone has already thought of that, and they are already trading under that business name, so try to think outside the box.

Create a New Shopify Account

Shopify has made this step extremely easy. All you have to do is go to the Shopify homepage. At that page, you will find a field where you have to enter your email address to start the process. Once you have entered the address, click the "get started" button. You will then be asked to create a password and input your chosen store name. Shopify will ask you a few questions about how much experience you have had in the e-commerce sector, and then they will ask you to provide a few accurate personal details. After you are done providing those details, your account will be officially opened, and you can then proceed to optimize your settings.

Set Up Your Account and Add All Necessary Information

You have to go through your new account's settings one menu item at a time, and you are going to input the information you need to configure your account before it can be operational. You have to put in place the correct settings to allow you to receive customer payments, to create your shipping rates, and to establish your store policies.

Dropshipping

When customizing your account, your first task will be to add one or more payment options to your store. Unless you have this in place, there will be no way for your customers to pay you for the products they'll purchase. Go to your Shopify settings page and click on the tab that has the word "payment" on it. You will have the option to add a PayPal account or to use other payment solutions.

We highly recommend that you use PayPal because it's extremely convenient and it has a deep market penetration, so most people who shop online already have PayPal accounts of their own. You can also opt for other payment systems if you find them convenient or necessary given the particular nature of your products (for example, if yours is a store that mostly sells products to offices and other businesses, you may find it more convenient to add a payment system that allows for bank transfers.

After you have all your payment channels in place, it's time to set your store policies. These policies will govern the relationship between you and your customers, so you should make sure that they are clearly stated and that they are compliant with the law.

Shopify understands exactly what kind of policies you might need for your store, so they have created a tool that enables you to automatically generate store policies that are standardized. You can immediately generate a refund policy, a privacy policy, and even a set of terms and conditions that will protect your store from legal liability in many foreseeable situations. To gain access to the policy creation tool, you have to click on the "checkout" tab, the go through the page to find each of the fields that you have to fill. You can then click on the "generate" button, and your policy will be set.

When your customers check out after making a purchase, the full text of the policy will appear, and they'll have to accept those terms and conditions before the sale goes through. If you have your own conditions that you want to include in the policy, there are some templates that you can use as guides to create your own policy.

Finally, you will have to declare your shipping rates. Many e-commerce experts recommend that you should account for the shipping price when you mark up the price of each item in the store, and then, you should offer your customers "free shipping." This is a marketing technique that works pretty well because it makes most customers believe that they are getting a great deal, so they'll be more inclined to go through with the purchase. You can click on the 'Shipping' button and select your preferred shipping options for different zones, starting with domestic ones and proceeding all the way to international zones.

Launch Your Dropshipping Store

After you are done with your settings and configurations, you should proceed to launch your new dropshipping store. To do this, click on the "sales channels" option, and then click on "Add sales channel." When you are done with that step, you will have a real online business that is up and running.

Design and Personalize Your Store

Now that you own an online store, it's time to personalize it. Here, you have to consider how you want your customers to view your site as they browse through it and make purchases. The design of your shop is going to be crucial, and it may have a huge bearing on your level of success as a drop-shipper. You want to make a good first impression when customers visit your site, and you want to project an image of professionalism. The two most important design aspects that you have to consider are the theme and the logo of your shop.

Shopify has a large collection of themes in their inbuilt theme store, so you don't have to worry about finding a theme that suits your brand. You can use a free theme option, or you can pay a little money for a premium theme. If you are working under a tight budget, a free theme will do just fine. However, if you are very particular about your branding, you may want to go for a premium theme. Try out a few themes before you settle on one. After selecting a theme, you can customize it to make it more reflective of your brand.

Logos are important for branding purposes because they enable customers to remember your dropshipping store in case they want to make more purchases in the future. Your logo should blend with other design aspects of your shop because you want to create a sense of uniformity.

You can use tools like the Oberlo Logo Maker to create a high-quality logo in a matter of minutes. All you have to do is play around with colors, fonts, and icons. If you are a skilled graphics designer, you can create your own logo and upload it onto your Shopify account. You can also hire graphic design experts for cheap on sites like Fiverr and Upwork. After you are done with both the logo and the design of your store, it's time to add your products.

Add Products to Your Store

To add a product to your shop, go to Shopify Admin and click on "Products." You should then click on the "Add a Product" button on the top right part of the page.

You will then have access to fields where you can enter the title and the description of your product. Fill the fields by either copying and pasting the text from your supplier's website or adding a description that you have prepared on your own. Make sure that you use colorful language in your product description because your customers are going to make purchase decisions based on that description.

You should then scroll down the page and find the "Images" section. Here, you have the option of adding images by uploading image files from your computer. You can also use "drag and drop" to achieve the same outcome. Make sure you upload your favorite product image first because it's the one that is going to act as a "featured image," meaning that it will appear prominently on the sales page when your customers scroll through your shop.

You should then review all your product details, particularly the "visibility" settings to make sure that your product is set to appear on the online store. You should also review the "Organization" settings and modify them to make sure your product is properly categorized according to Vendor, Product Type, and Collections.

You then have to input the price of the product. As you do that, you can select an option that makes it possible for customers to compare prices, and you can also check a box that allows a tax to be added to the final price of the product.

When you get to the inventory section, you should add your SKU, your Inventory Policy, and a Barcode. Indicate whether or not your product has a shipping price, then select the weight bracket of the product. If your product comes in different sizes and colors, you should fill the "Variants" section appropriately, and put in the different prices for each variant.

Finally, you should edit your Meta Title and Meta Description in order to improve your SEO (search engine optimization) so that customers will have an easier time finding your product online. Ensure that you save all your product information correctly and that you view your product listing from the front end to see it from the point of view of the customer. You should repeat all these steps to add more products, or you can use services such as Oberlo which can help you add products to your account automatically.

Start Selling and Cashing in

Now that everything is done, you can start making sales. Remember that dropshipping is a competitive business, so you should do everything that you can to promote your products on blogs, social media, and other websites. Advertising is also an option if you have the resources.

CHAPTER 8

How to Market your products

Nobody will see the items you have in your store as a dropshipper from Shopify unless you sell them vigorously. If you have to market, get ready to go out and let people know about the items you've got in your store. Now, you can advertise your store and drive or generate traffic in several ways. We're going to look at some of those ways in this section. We typically have two main ways to drive a store's traffic—organic and paid traffic.

This is a good example of organic traffic when you post on your social media timeline about the products you have in your store and leave a link to the store or product page. You don't care for it. When you make guest posts on blogs and include a connection to your store in the call-to-action section, you can also get free or organic traffic.

One issue with strategies for the production of free or subsidized traffic is that they require time to produce outcomes, and the outcome only trickles in like water. Unless you're a big influence on social media, it shouldn't be your best option to focus on sources of organic traffic. Rather, by paying for traffic, you should make your results easier.

Facebook PPC (pay per click advertising) is one of the main traffic drivers for dropshipping. What makes it great is that you'll get huge traffic in your store if you do it well. Facebook ads, as they are often named, encourage you to target individuals who are actively interested in the types of products you market.

It doesn't leave you space to blindly speculate–within a certain group; you can target people; you can target people residing in a specific area. You can also hit anyone who, in the last few months or weeks, have purchased something online.

On almost any other online platform, Facebook captures user data, and that's the info they use to enhance their advertising plans. Another great feature of Facebook ads is that when someone views or clicks on the message, you will still be paid. It's not like some other forms of advertisement where you are paid whether or not viewers see the advertisements.

Facebook won't charge you if people don't see your ads, so it's a win-win for you. Interestingly, running Facebook ads is cheap–you can run high conversion ads with as little as $5, and send a lot of traffic to your store. You're going to spend on the advertising and the big traffic you're going to get when you compare the amount, so Facebook ads are worth it.

Here are the measures you can take to operate Facebook ads: Note: making strongly transformed Facebook ads is a path on its own–and this topic is not something we can cover. If you are interested in learning more about how to operate successful advertising, consider getting some materials on the topic. What we're trying to bring here to you is just the help you need.

Stage 1: Build a Facebook page – for operating Facebook ads, you need a Facebook page. You can't use your personal Facebook page to run ads. Make sure that the page name represents the type of products you market while designing a website.

Step 2: Go to your page, and click on "Ad center," then "create ad."

You will be required to give a name to your advertisement and mention what you want your ad to achieve. There are choices for you to choose from–would you like to increase your page's exposure? Would you like to direct traffic to an outside channel such as a website or e-commerce store? You will see a lot of options from which you can pick.

Step3: Choose your target audience – you can set up your ad to only see viewers in a certain place. You can also set up advertisements so that advertising can only be seen by people who earn a certain revenue limit.

Step 4: Creative ad and ad copy – ad creative is the image or video that accompanies an ad. People prefer to use videos as a creative ad–the logic is that videos have a better conversion ratio than images. You can use photographs as well. Make sure that whatever you use as your innovative ad is relevant to your business. Yes, if you use an illustration, it should be a picture of the product you advertise. To have the frustrated Facebook user swipe down their page to pause and check, it should be enticing enough.

The text that follows the ad picture is your ad copy–you use it to illustrate to the audience what's in it. If your ad text isn't compelling enough or you don't have a lot of Facebook user benefits, they won't bother clicking what you're advertising.

A good way to learn how to write ad copies is to start watching some of the various Facebook ads that show on your Facebook timeline from time to time. Look out for ads any time you click through Facebook and see how the marketers produced their copy and the kind of creativity they used. This will help you learn how to make your own ad copies to create the best artistic ad.

Step 5: Set your budget – Facebook allows you to set or determine how much you would like to spend running an ad every day. If you want to spend only $5, you can set it. Facebook will not charge you more than your daily budget.

Once the ad has been set up and personalized, post the ad and wait for the Facebook team's approval. The ad would usually be checked to make sure it follows all requirements. If you followed the instructions, your ad should be accepted as soon as possible.

You can then sit back and watch the traffic coming to your store once the ad has been approved. Use different ad sets to create more ad campaigns and learn the one that performs better. This is also single checking of A / B. Stick to it once you've found the ad sets that give you the best performance.

Remember, the above steps are just an overview–learning how to run effective Facebook ads, as mentioned earlier, is a course on its own. To broaden your knowledge, you might consider getting some materials on the topic. You'll also know more about how to tailor and automate the ad for better results while you continue to run your ads.

Other means of driving traffic to your store

Using Instagram influencers

Instagram has progressively moved from being a platform for photo-sharing to a powerful marketing tool. Since then, companies have found that they can draw more clients simply by sharing on Instagram about their business.

What makes Instagram perfect is that a number of monthly users are getting in. Over 800 million people are currently visiting the platform on a monthly basis. Will you know the meaning of that? Several people will be revealing your business.

One thing that makes Instagram unique is that the secret value of Instagram as a marketing tool is still to be seen by other business owners. Many of these advertisers still see Instagram as a photo-sharing platform that is only suitable for sharing pictures of their holidays.

Many advertisers are still searching it out for Snapchat marketing purposes on WhatsApp. But if you're going to take your business to Instagram, you're going to be among the early birds that will use the site to log huge sales.

There are three approaches you may advertise the store on Instagram:

- Build a huge following
- Air Instagram advertising–close to Facebook ads
- Pay Instagram influencers to endorse the brand

This takes time to build a massive audience on Instagram–you may need to spend months to do so. Often, to maintain your audience, you will need to regularly post useful content. This may seem like a long process to the typical dropshipper who just wants to send traffic to their store and make money. For such a dropshipper, the other choices are to display Instagram ads.

Although it takes time to grow a following on Instagram, and it won't give you instant results, you still have to do it. That's how to do it– whether operating Instagram ads or partnering with influencers, make sure you create your own follow-up at the same time. By the time your following has expanded to a reasonable number, you could stop working with influencers and start posting content for ads directly on your website.

While waiting for your audience to expand, start with Instagram advertising–it's just like running Facebook ads. You pick your target audience, you set up an innovative ad and replicate them, you set your schedule, and you're ready to go. Instagram ads are growing, if not stronger, just like Facebook ads. It can be a huge source of traffic to your store if it is set up correctly.

You should partner with an Instagram influencer to help you drive traffic to your store apart from the two solutions above.

Who's an Instagram influencer?

An Instagram influencer is just an Instagram user whose content they share on the platform has grown considerably. Influencers also record huge commitments on their posts—so it's clear that you'll get good results if you pay them to market your product. Anyone with up to 50k followers might typically be considered an influencer.

Influencer marketing, which involves paying influencers to sell a business, started to become common as many people's lives began to focus on social media. Influencer marketing is now perceived to be a legitimate way to market a product or service. In the coming years, it will also continue to be relevant.

Another thing that works well for influencer marketing is that people who follow influencers see them as a leader and would be able to do something that they were requested to do by the power. Influencers are seen as more knowledgeable people on a topic, and their followers obey their advice when they suggest a product or service.

Use the search feature for Instagram to locate an influencer in your niche. Check for users with a huge following in your niche. Observe their patterns of posting and how many people are involved with their posts. Go through their posts and see if, in the past, they helped people post sponsored content. Write a direct message to the influencer and let them know that you'd like to partner with them.

You need to be vigilant when looking for an influencer, so you don't pay anybody with fake followers for money. How do you know a follower of someone? It's easy—considered the number of their followers interacting with their articles and juxtapose them with their number of followers. For, e.g., if someone has 100k followers and less than 100 people are interacting with their posts, it goes to show you that most followers are created by a bot.

You don't want someone whose posts don't record a lot of commitment to pay money. Many unethical people are paying money to get bot-generated followers on Instagram—make sure you're not working with people like this, its a waste of your time.

Give them a direct message if you've completed your due diligence and picked an influencer to partner with. Let them think that you want to give them a yell. Negotiate with the influencer with the quality following and give them the promotional profile you want to advertise. In order to get the advertised product, the influencer will include a connection to your store to their bio and encourage their fans to click the link.

Make sure that the influencer does not make the ad post sound too salesy when collaborating with an influencer. Alternatively, you'd like them to build the article in a manner that seems they're only trying to suggest a product they've used before.

The shoutout post can stay on the influencer's page for a day, week, month, or several months, based on your agreement with the influencer. The price you'll pay for the ad to live for one day on an influencer's page will vary from the cost you'll pay for the one-month post.

How much is paid by an influencer? There's no fixed amount for the influencer. The price you're going to pay hinges on so many things like your negotiation capacity, the influencer involved, how many days you want the post to stay up, and even the type of product you're selling. The expense of influencer marketing is not going to dig a hole in your pocket on average, and the findings can be quite promising. Most dropshippers utilize marketing power to drive traffic to their stores.

CHAPTER 9

Tools That You Need For Your Store

I n this rapidly changing world, no business can survive without using certain online tools. These provide assurance to the business when trends change and act as a backbone whenever any support is required. The convenience that using an online tool provides is incomparable to other manual forms. Whether it is making calculations for inventory or to make business expansion plans, technology plays the biggest and most significant role. Productivity and efficiency have increased by a lot, especially in the past decade as businesses of all sizes have had the opportunity to update its online services. The constant need to be updated with changing technology is essential for businesses to be able to attract new customers with ease.

Creating your e-commerce store

To explore the potential of your store, you need to be ready to adapt to all the available platforms, which will ensure the sustainability of your business. Before even looking all of the options available to make your store stand out, creating an e-commerce store is the first step. It is a necessity to have sound knowledge in technology and the online tools that are out there to start. There are professionals who can set the store up for you, as well as websites solely dedicated to help out beginners like you. Do not hesitate to seek help! These platforms are very well suited to e-commerce entrepreneurs who are just starting out. Moreover, these applications can guide you through steps to manage almost everything when launching your store.

Picking a theme

Now comes the part where you need to focus on particular and intricate details of your niche that will define your e-commerce store. However, before this step, you need to have good knowledge of the type of products you want to work with. The very inspiration for having a relevant theme that portrays your vision comes from your product range. If you are seeking help from a professional website or application, you will find a lot of preset themes there already. These can help you in brainstorming ideas and making decisions if you are unsure where to start. More importantly, think about customizing your store and giving it a unique touch. In a lot of cases, generic designs can be a turn off to consumers, while innovative ones can entice high-end customers and turn them into returning customers in the long run.

Designing an e-commerce store

Whenever customers visit your store, the theme, color palette and the design are the first things that they notice. At times, you may wonder, "Why do I need to put an extra effort into making it pretty?" or "Isn't having a great range of products enough?" Well, the answer is simple - if consumers are not interested, they will not bother going through whatever your store has to offer. Having an aesthetically pleasing e-commerce store entices customers and also validates your business as a professional one. With word of mouth, more people can become aware of and take notice of your store. If it is unorganized or shabby, it would be very difficult for you to attract them. Hence, to have and maintain loyal and potential customers, investing your resources on building a good e-commerce store is a necessity.

Online Logo Makers

After you have designed and set your store up, now is the time to brand it. This helps to gain recognition for your products and creates a lasting first impression in the minds of the customers. It can be anything from a simple tree to an intricate design; this should depend on the type of products you are selling. It is better to be more open to ideas and new designs instead of being adamant on one. Having a professional store can do wonders and help create a buzz among customers. Hence, a logo is the simplest and best solution for you to put your business out there. If you want to experiment, do not shy away from creating your own design but if you are not proficient enough, do not shy away from help from online logo makers. Hiring graphic designers or outsourcing can be great options too, depending on the budget you have for creating the logo.

Payment processing

Due to globalization, we have access to faster services, much faster than those in the past. The systems for making online payments have developed immensely and have made it easier for us to make daily purchases. You do not need to carry cash around all the time. Their personal information and details are encrypted and have protection from credit card frauds for when businesses are willing to adopt such models. You should do research on the most common online methods of making payment among your targeted customers and make sure that you provide them with those payment services. PayPal is one of the most efficient systems in the most recent times. You can also be open towards offline payment services but the online payment methods are much more convenient in today's time.

Online business plan services

If you are happy with your strategies and find that they are working for your business, this should not be a tool you need. However, it is recommended that you explore these services. An outside perspective is necessary for you to be able to work on your shortcomings. For entrepreneurs, these online plans for your business guide you in designing a feasible and strong plan when you are making the transition from great idea to a profitable business venture. The inbuilt features and tool templates of web based applications help you generate charts on performance and goal achievement. Your financial status, depending on investments made for the business, can be studied carefully. You can be in charge of and keep track of the progress that you are making. Once you learn about what the services offer you, it would not be a surprise to see that you have started to think more critically and that your ideas for your store and product line go beyond the surface.

Using social media for your store

Whether you want to focus on Facebook, Instagram, Twitter, or any other social networking website, engagement with your customers through this platform is one of the most effective ways to draw and drive traffic to your store. Using social media is attractive as you do not have to invest a lot of money into it and you can utilize it to broaden your reach. Millions of people all around the world can engage with your store. Specialized tools on individual platforms are available to make social media users aware of new products and you have the flexibility to promote your products and content related to them. This also helps you to create a brand for your store. The best part is that as more time passes by, these platforms continue to grow and once you can get comfortable with social media, you should expect to look at great numbers!

Web hosting

The pace of the business world is much faster than what it was ten years ago. You cannot expect to apply those same strategies for attracting customers today. Hence, if you have not explored the internet yet, you will lag behind and before you realize, you will already be out of the game. A web hosting service allows you to start a website and run it. The files that makeup the website on a data server can be stored through these services and these files are uploaded to the web automatically from your web hosting service. The use of email marketing and installation of one-click supported applications are some of the many features that you can use when building your business. You can also be assigned an email address that includes the site's domain name.

Shopping cart software

When you have set up your website, there are some additional things which you need to offer your customers when they make a purchase. Shopping cart software is necessary to be able to make payments through your website. This is not only beneficial for the customers as it can allow them to feel safe when buying something online, but it is an advantage for your store too. Tracking inventory gets easier and you can keep tabs on which product to promote or communicate with the suppliers if a surge is predicted with the latest trends. This will also help you produce reports based on this data through your website's services. This software can be connected to multiple platforms for making payments. PayPal or credit card services can be offered to customers and this makes their experience more familiar as well. The purchasers can also be aware of the amount of tax they are paying and how much they are being charged for shipping costs. You promote transparency and convenience through these services on your store's website and it will help you gain a good reputation among old and new customers.

Webinar services

As your business grows, you may think of expanding and gaining new customers, both locally and internationally. Webinar services can help you connect and take orders faster and most importantly, they can help you monitor your day to day operations, especially if you have multiple offices. This will help you out if your employees are working remotely and if you have multiple working locations. Training sessions, meetings with all of your employees, either within a specific branch or all together, can be conducted much more comfortably. Webinar services are a great fit for you when you want to present your sales online and make product demonstrations for your clients too. Becoming more proficient in this helps you connect with your customers faster and you can respond to their queries in real time.

Anti-virus software

When you are using your computer, it is highly likely that you are storing information through a variety of applications. Whether you are dealing with storing personal information or you are processing orders, you need to keep all the data in an organized way. The information stored here is valuable and not having any protection programs on your computer puts you and your business in a lot of danger. Apart from the technical issues that your computer will go through, you could experience data theft, which would be a very big loss for your business venture. All businesses should have anti-virus software to guard the computer network against viruses, malware, Trojans, worms, or spyware. Since the platform of dropshipping is online where you have to constantly be in touch with your suppliers and customers, having a good antivirus software is a necessity and it is equally necessary for protection.

Receiving payments from customers

In order to deal with customers from various backgrounds, your knowledge in different modes of payment platforms is required. It reduces hassle if you can connect to multiple platforms that your customers will feel safe using. There are additional charges when you want to use these online payment platforms, ensuring to keep you safe against business fraud. You will be charged a fee for every sale you make and an additional amount to ensure protection for your store. You should check out different platforms apart from PayPal to make a sound decision, however, it is and has been the most trusted and convenient one in the market. Apart from this, there are built-in features to provide you protection if you are using platforms like Shopify.

Online data storage

Due to the ease of an online platform, storing data has become much easier than it used to be. Online data storage acts as backup storage if anything goes wrong with your computer. Of course, you can access your data online even if no problems arise instead of relying on your computer's storage. Data is stored on a cloud server which is convenient and safe. You can access the files from any part of the world at any time. Also, if you want to free up space on your computer, having online data storage is the best way to go about this. It is wiser to have online storage as hard drive failures, theft, and file erasure can occur and make these files extremely difficult to retrieve.

Business tools that you should know how to use

Google AdWords & Analytics

Google is the place we think of going instantly whenever there is something we want to know. From getting instant information about the most complicated technologies to doing the most basic spell checks, Google is our one-stop solution. For your business, you need to learn to make the most of this platform. Whenever you want to know about anything, this search engine can give you around 40,000 results per second and is definitely the most reliable search engine today. You can focus on getting on the first page of the search list and witness how this changes your income. Use an SEO (search engine optimization) strategy to try and make it on the first page. It may take a long time, maybe even months or longer, but you should keep at it. This will ensure you benefits in the long term. However, there is another way that can help you attain a first-page position faster, and this strategy includes using Google AdWords. This is a scheme of paid ads where you pay every time a visitor clicks on your advertisement. Additionally, you need to invest time into how to utilize Google Analytics and understand its importance for your website and your business. This tool allows you to understand the types of mediums through which your visitors come from and this could be a huge advantage when you are starting out or are struggling to reinvent your line. Overall, this will assist with things that are working and not working, guiding you towards better execution and expansion plans.

SurveyMonkey

Now that you have set your store up and are getting ready to attract customers to your niche, you need to know about the current market and what the trends are. This is a surveying tool available online that helps you connect with your audience. Survey Monkey already has a lot of preset questions along with built-in templates to give you a thorough insight when analyzing data. The best aspect is that the tool gives unbiased responses which can help you modify your strategies or help you create new and improved ones. The free version of this tool still provides you a lot of information through the surveys but the number of features is limited. Give it a try and see how much it helps improve your product line. If you are finding it useful, go ahead and get a subscription with a paid plan. The paid plan will provide many more useful tools for surveying.

X-Cart

For newcomers who do not have a lot of money to start out but want to give dropshipping a shot, your e-commerce website still needs to stand out. This tool is cost-effective and will not put a strain on your funds. X-Cart has a free version if you want to give it a try and see whether you find it suitable for your business or not. It helps you build your website and you can explore its various features. Moreover, free extensions will allow you to create shipping labels, slideshows, and do so much more! Your business can access these facilities and prioritize what will be more beneficial to get started on in terms of harnessing technical skills. You can get acquainted with the different themes available online and customize them wherever you feel necessary.

Tableau Public

This is a marketing tool that helps you to conduct research and lets you make a thorough analysis of your business data. You learn to make better predictions on what will work and what will not and this helps you make better decisions for the future. This tool is very effective because it sources out data from CSV files and Excel among many others. When the business venture is new, investing in high profile marketing research tools is important but expensive. This is where this tool is handiest as it can give free access to up to 15 million rows in one workbook and provide data solutions for free with up to 10 gigabytes of space.

BuzzSumo

In the modern day, social media has been the best platform for marketing. Social media is perfect for if you want to understand demographics, connect with influencers, find out what the most shared content is and much more. BuzzSumo is the best influencer marketing tool that allows you to find out what content is performing the best on any social media platform. You can choose a paid subscription but there is a free trial period too which you should definitely make use of before making a purchase. This application helps you understand what sort of content will work well with your product line; this in turn will help you connect with influencers who can help you in expanding your marketing strategies.

CHAPTER 10

Create your brand and build your audience

Assuming you already have a website and an audience, you can skip this chapter. Otherwise, it is vital that you continue reading to make sure your brand is aligned with your business model and the product you are selling. A good start-up point is to ask what exactly a brand is. A brand is much more than a simple logo and is rather an ethos, a mission and a commercial approach. That logo simply tells people that the product or service they are receiving meets the same standards as anything they have used in the past. Start your brand by choosing why you do what you do. Why should people care about your company? How is it different from other companies that offer the same? How do you want the world to change, after your company is part of it? This is what allows a company like Apple to capture the imagination of billions of people and create such loyal customers.

Apple not only cares about selling hardware but also about creating beautiful, personal, and highly targeted hardware for creative people who break the rules compared to large companies. When the first Apple computer was launched, the only competition was IBM and by taking this position, Apple was able to differentiate itself a lot and excite many followers accordingly. The same is true for many companies that want to create a greener planet. These companies are doing more than just making money and their fans love it. This is enough for people to choose their products instead of the same products offered by another company. These two companies could sell exactly the same product, but the way they do it is completely different. And if you can convey this mission statement, you will find that the right type of customer will go absolutely crazy about your brand. This is the type of customer whose vision is aligned with his. Don't try to attract everyone who will never work. Instead, try to attract more to the right kind of person.

Create your logo

You can do it in two ways, designing it yourself or hiring someone to design it for you. The goal of a great logo is to communicate what your business is about. You are trying to tell people what you sell and why you sell it as soon as they look at your business. Suppose your company focuses on natural and health products, so you could create a logo with a tree or a heart. It would probably be green and have an edifying and healthy name. On the contrary, if your business is to punish gymnastics workouts, your logo may include an image of a handlebar and have the word iron somewhere. The idea is that the combination of your logo, company name and perhaps blog posts is enough to tell any visitor to your site immediately that this is a company that runs them exactly and they will love it. This should also extend to site design. In the meantime, make sure your logo is designed using a vector file (which means it is made in Illustrator or similar software that simplifies editing and resizing) and avoids the use of clichés. Again, this is a good place to invest some of your money in advance that you will pay largely in the long term.

Build your audience and build trust

This is the basic concept of content marketing to create an audience of people who love their content and trust their opinion so you can convince them to buy the products you recommend and so you can continue to attract people to your site from time to time. From time to time, offering you more opportunities to make a sale. The way to do it is to start writing high-quality content and publish it on a blog on a regular basis. The more you write and the more you research your topic and make it different and interesting, the faster you will create a dedicated audience to which you can sell. Show that you really know what you are talking about, that you only recommend things that you sincerely believed in and that your audience can rely on you as a resource for more useful ideas and information. Similarly, try to build your mailing list and your presence on social networks. Firmly incorporate your brand into all social media pages and anything else you create, so people know they are dealing with the same business. Making someone follow you on social media when they think they are interested in your brand is much easier than letting them buy you a product and spend money! Meanwhile, your social media accounts will help you attract more new customers to your site by allowing people to share with your network. You can also help by providing buttons to share on social networks that will allow people who like your content on Facebook or Tweet on Twitter. Only after you have generated a large audience of people who regularly visit your site, you should start thinking about introducing products on your page. If you have really created a brand that you believe in and if you have provided real value to your content, you should discover that you have real fans. And true fans will be desperate to buy your products when you start selling them!

Other ways to promote your products

Of course, there are many additional methods you can use to send more customers to your products and market your store. One option is to create your own affiliate program and encourage more people to help market your items. Another method is to pay for advertising if it's a pay-per-click campaign through Google AdWords or if it's a highly targeted Facebook ad for your specific demographic. Both will be explained vividly later in this book, so don't worry too much about it now. It works well in scenarios where it sells from eBay or Amazon and is not trying to create an audience. If you intend to pay for advertising, you must calculate the LCV (Customer lifetime value) of each customer. This will allow you to ensure that, regardless of what you spend on your ads, earn more, and see a solid ROI.

CHAPTER 11

Mistakes To Avoid When Starting The Business

Here are some common mistakes that many novice drop-shippers tend to make. We will discuss why people find themselves making these mistakes, and what you should do to avoid making them:

Starting Without Learning the Ins and Outs of Dropshipping

There has been much hype around the topic of dropshipping, and a lot of misinformation came along with it. Many self-proclaimed "dropshipping gurus" have been telling people how easy it is to start a dropshipping business, and this has led a lot of people to assume that you don't need to learn any technical aspects of the business to succeed. The truth is that the dropshipping game is evolving pretty fast, and there is stiff competition in every niche, so you should avoid jumping into the business without taking a little time to learn as much as you can about the trade.

Choosing Bad Suppliers

Many newbies fail to look into the history of suppliers to find out if they have a reputation for unreliability. They assume that in order to maximize their profits, they need to go with the supplier who offers the lowest prices, but the truth is that the quality of service and the reliability of a supplier is much more important for a drop-shipper than saving a few cents on each order. If a supplier messes up and makes a lot of excuses during your first few weeks of operation, you should drop him and find a more reliable one before your business gets stuck with a bunch of negative reviews.

Lacking Faith in the Dropshipping Model

For you to succeed as a drop-shipper, you have to stick to the model. Some first-timers make the mistake of doubting how the model works, so they try to blend dropshipping with other forms of retail e-commerce. This often happens when newbie drop-shippers worry about their suppliers running out of stock, so they go out and use their own money to buy some inventory. If you have chosen to be a drop-shipper, you should stick with it and concentrate on scaling your business, and you should avoid complicating things unnecessarily. Have faith that the system will work.

Expecting Money to Come Easily

Again, the notion that dropshipping brings in quick and easy money comes from the so-called experts who misinform people because of their own personal agendas. As a drop-shipper, don't assume that you will set up a store, launch it, then sit back and start watching the money flow in. Success in dropshipping requires hard work, proactivity, and a competitive attitude. Customers don't just come to your shop, you have to go out there on the internet, find them and bring them in through advertising and content marketing. Dropshipping is not a get rich quick scheme.

Failing to Retarget Your Site Visitors

Retargeting site visitors is probably the most effective marketing strategy out there in terms of the sales that it generates. If you don't take advantage of retargeting ads on Facebook or Google, that's akin to throwing money away. People visit a shopping site or a sales page because on some level, they really would like to buy that product, so if you keep reminding them about it, one day, as soon as they can get some money, they are highly likely to come back and make that purchase. If you have limited marketing funds, make retargeting ads a priority in your marketing strategy.

Using Low-Quality Product Images

First-time drop-shippers are encouraged to use free photos as a cost-cutting measure, but that doesn't mean that you should use low-resolution product photos. If your supplier provides low-quality photos, try to find better photos of the product elsewhere online, or you can order a sample of the product and take your own photos of it. Online shoppers don't get to see the products they are buying beforehand, so they rely on photos to make purchase decisions. To be fully convinced about the quality of a product, most of them would want to see lots of high-resolution photos from different angles so that they can zoom in and study the product in detail.

Misleading Your Customers About Your Shipping Time

Many new drop-shippers are afraid that the customer might go elsewhere if they think that the shipping time for a product is too long. Some drop-shippers are tempted to either conceal the real shipping time or to straight up lie about it. If you can't guarantee fast shipping for a certain product, you should be honest about it, and offer an explanation as to why it's taking longer than expected (perhaps you are shipping it from abroad). Misleading customers about your shipping time counts as terrible customer service, and if a customer has to wait longer for a package that he was promised, he is highly likely to take his business elsewhere.

Being Afraid to Reinvest Your Money in the Business

When dropshipping novices make a little money from their businesses at the beginning, some are usually afraid of putting the money back into the business for fear that they could end up losing it all. However, the right approach is to reinvest at least some of the money you make into the business through adverting or SEO. There are lots of ways to advertise one's dropshipping business—you could hire influencers, buy PPC ads, etc. Your business won't grow if you take every cent you make out of it. Use your proceeds to scale your business in order to make more profits.

Failing to Work with Instagram Influencers

Right now, Instagram is one of the hottest platforms if you are looking to advertise any kind of product. People follow influencers on Instagram to an almost religious extent, and you would be surprised at how many people will be willing to buy a product just because one influencer mentioned it. You can easily find an influencer within your niche who is willing to give your store or product a shout out for a bit of cash. The bigger you dream, the bigger you'll grow, so don't be afraid to spend a lump sum of cash for an endorsement from a few powerful influencers.

Using Complicated Shipping Fee Structures

First-time drop-shippers tend to publish complicated shipping fee structures on their websites or to display shipping fees under the price tag of every item in their shops. This can be confusing and off-putting for many customers. Customers don't need to see your cost breakdowns, they just want to know how much the whole thing is going to cost them. Instead of having separate shipping fees for all listed items, you should just set prices that account for shipping costs and then offer free shipping. This is a neat marketing trick that can make customers think that you are offering them a great deal.

Creating Unclear Policies

Many novice drop-shippers make the mistake of thinking that store policies are mere formalities, so they fail to make them as clear as necessary. You should avoid having unclear policies. If you don't know how to create such policies, you can borrow ideas from other similar businesses, or you can use online tools provided by industry players such as Shopify. For example, if you don't explicitly state in your policies that a customer has to include a tracking number when returning a package, and then the customer claims that he sends back the package without producing a tracking number to prove it, you won't have any recourse if the package "gets lost in the mail."

Mishandling Product Returns

Product returns are complicated and frustrating for drop-shippers because they require a lot of correspondence, and they cost money. However, they are also an opportunity for you to deliver good customer service, and they help you learn the weaknesses in your system so that you can fix them. Many first-time drop-shippers mishandle product returns by trying to shortchange the customer or by taking their frustrations out on the supplier. You have to remember that returns are part of the business and in the end, they are inevitable. You should prepare for them by outlining clear rules on how they ought to be handled and by sticking to those rules even if things get frustrating.

Relying Too Much on One Supplier

Many drop-shippers make the mistake of counting too much on a single supplier. This leaves them unprepared in case anything unexpected happens. You should always have several backup suppliers for every product in your store. If something happens, say your supplier runs out of stock or hikes up his prices, you can count on your backups to fill your orders. If you are in a situation where your business could live or die depending on the actions of a single supplier, then you are not managing your risks properly.

Failing to Test Several Products

You may have a niche in mind when you start your business, and you may select great products that bring in a decent profit, but that shouldn't be the end of it, you should keep testing new products to see if you can make money off of them. If you are inflexible about the products that you carry in your store, you could wake up one day to find that there is a universal shortage of your best-selling product, so it's good to have backup products. By testing several products, you can identify those that may come in handy when you want to scale your business.

Focusing on Price Competition

Many first-time drop-shippers make the mistake of thinking that they can beat out the competition by setting their prices lower than everyone else. While it's true that customers like bargains and low prices, there are other more sustainable ways to make your store stand out from the competition. If you start a price war, you will be digging your own grave. Whenever businesses start undercutting each other, it's the ones that have few resources that end up losing. You cannot undercut dominant online retailers because they are always willing to match the lowest price, so you have to differentiate yourself by offering great service with a personal touch.

Selling Products That Violate Trademark or Copyright Laws

Just because a supplier has a product available in his inventory doesn't mean that it is entirely legal. There are many cases where suppliers stock knockoff products that are often imported from Asia. You may also see clothes or accessories with nice logos from popular Western franchises and decide to sell them in your store. You should be extremely careful in these situations because some of those products may violate the legal rights of other businesses, and you could get sued by the companies that own the trademarks, copyrights, or other intellectual properties that were used to make those products.

CHAPTER 12

How to Scale Your Dropshipping Business

S caling is vital for the success of a dropshipping business. Without growth, your business will stagnate, and that is the beginning of the end of any business. No matter what your personal goals are for your business, whether you want to become a business mogul or settle in and have a comfortable and sustainable business, you have to scale. The whole concept of scaling can be unnerving as you will be moving out of your comfort zone and taking on more responsibilities. However, if you go about scaling your business step-by-step and use all the tools and strategies available, it becomes easy to do and exciting to see your business grow.

Scaling is not a single option only way of growing your business. It is very flexible and if one particular form of scaling does not work for your niche, you have a variety of other options to try out and implement those that fit your particular dropshipping business the best. That is what makes scaling so successful, you can add all the different options that fit, there are no limits.

Are You Ready?

Premature scaling is the phrase used in commerce for expanding your business without first putting into place a solid foundation to build your scaling for your business. It is not only startup businesses that fall into this trap, even long established companies and this invariably leads to failure.

Before you can be ready to scale, you must work through several steps for your scaling efforts to be successful as follows.

Cash Safety Net

Build up a cash safety net for your business before you scale to allow for any setbacks during scaling. This will allow you to change strategies during scaling and have the cash to back you up if one strategy does not work out. Without a cash safety net, you won't have the means to try more than one strategy to get the perfect product and market fit.

Logical Steps Forward

You need to take the steps from the start to the implementation stage of scaling in the correct order. Starting at the wrong end of your scaling will result in a lot more work, money spent needlessly and opportunities lost.

Once you have committed to the scaling process you become less flexible to maneuver as you have started spending money on products, hiring a person or people to help run the business and advertising.

To avoid all the problems of premature scaling is not difficult. Do not spend money on non-essentials, save all extra cash to enable you to progress without getting into a cash bind in the middle of scaling. Once you have that set up you make very sure that you know exactly what your customers want and have all the ways to reach potential customers and have set up strategies and advertising to reach all of your potential customers in the target group of your scaling effort. The last step is to test whatever products you want to scale, or new products you want to add to your business. You must base your scaling on proven test results, not guesses or what people say are the latest trends or fads. Once you have all the above in place, you have eliminated the possibility of premature scaling and are indeed ready to start scaling your dropshipping business.

Scaling Vertically

Traditional vertical scaling means you add more products in your niche or expand on the categories in your niche. You also increase your budget for advertising for existing ad sets that are doing extremely well. In short you offer more products, increase your ad spend, but do not focus on finding new audiences to target within your niche. This is a good, solid way of scaling with a proven track record.

Scaling Horizontally

Scaling horizontally give you several options, or combinations of the horizontal scaling options to implement, whichever fits your business best and you find the most comfortable to use. Basically, instead of scaling upwards with your existing products, you scale by introducing your products to new audiences – you scale wide.

Become Your Own Franchise

You duplicate your existing business and online store to open up the opportunity to sell to clients in your niche who speak another language. If you speak more than one language, you can manage this yourself by simply translating everything on your existing website to the target language.

If you do not speak another language, go into partnership with someone who speaks your target language and share profits for the new franchise website on a 50% basis with this person.

Duplicating your business in another language has greater appeal to people where the official language is not English. Shoppers in Europe, the Balkan countries and the Far East prefer to shop online in their own language and prefer the Euro as payment currency.

The benefit of duplicating is that you will have a higher conversion rate, but you also take on a lot more work and you will be limited in how many countries you can target in your scaling efforts.

Keep It English and Go Global

Scaling globally and keeping everything in English has the drawback of losing potential clients who do not want to do business in English and use USD as the currency for payment, giving you a lower conversion rate.

To offset this drawback, scale globally for the countries where English is the official language or one of the official languages. This form of global scaling is a lot less work than duplicating your website, freeing up time to concentrate on other areas of your business.

Scaling Into Neighboring Niches

This is a great way to scale your business, by investigating the niches that borders on your own niche and look for any products in these neighboring niches that would compliment the products that you are already selling. Look for products that the customers in your own niche would be interested in buying and test the reaction to the new products by offering a few at a time. Your sales statistics will clearly show you which products your niche customers like best and then you can make adjustments to the products you offer from neighboring niches.

You can do this form of scaling indefinitely without spending extra on advertising before you are sure that any neighboring niche products are viable to be added permanently.

Facebook Lookalike Audiences

Facebook offers a segmentation tool that creates lookalike audiences based on the followers that you currently have. The tool takes the interest and demographics of your followers to create a lookalike audience that you can target. As the demographics and interests of the new audience closely match that of your current followers, this form of scaling enables focussed marketing and finds you groups with a very high potential conversion rate.

Facebook uses its massive user base to look for similarities to create a lookalike audience that would never be found without the user data stored within Facebook. This tool works as long as you have a minimum of 100 people in your client group, but the larger your total is, the more effective this tool becomes.

You can create your lookalike audience from your customer lists, your website traffic and the fan pages you have and select different types of lookalike audiences.

Specific Demographics

You can refine your demographics for the lookalike audience by setting certain parameters such as specific location, gender, and age group for an even narrower focus to target your advertising.

Audience Size Selection

Select the large audience option to maximize the number of people you reach that similar to your current audience gives you a much broader audience, but there will be less similarities shared than your fans and current customers have in common.

When you select a smaller lookalike audience, it will result in a smaller number of people seeing your ads, but those people will share far more characteristics with your fans and clients.

Facebook CBO

In September 2019, Facebook introduced a new feature for optimizing how your advertising budget is distributed, the campaign budget optimization (CBO) feature. This algorithm now does real time optimization of your ad budget across your ad sets. It targets the best opportunities separately, optimizing them one-by-one on what it deems to be the least expensive cost per result. Once done with an opportunity, it moves on to the next best opportunity. It does not take into consideration the amount spent on the previous ad set. The benefit of CBO is that the algorithm targets your top performing ad sets and you no longer waste money on opportunities that are much less likely to lead to sales and conversions by intelligently optimizing your campaign budget to target the ads that perform the best and the audiences that respond the best.

Google Similar Audiences and Customer Match

Google offers several tools that assist you in re-engaging customers and scaling your business.

Customer Match uses your data, both offline and online, that customers have shared with you to enable you to re-engage customers across Display, YouTube, Search, Gmail, and Shopping. This tool can also target other potential clients similar to those you already have.

The Similar Audiences tool from Google, works on the same lines as the Facebook Lookalike tool. The searches for Similar Audiences most often uses your marketings lists, first-party data information to target new users who have share similar characteristics, and interests of your best performing website visitors groups.

Estimate and Plan

Planning ahead is crucial for scaling to be successful. To enable you to plan with accuracy, you must do two specific forecast evaluations. It is important to be as thorough as possible with as much data as possible to give you the best realistic results.

A customer growth forecast, broken down into categories with specifics such as number of new clients, estimated number of orders and broken down by different months.

An expense forecast on similar lines as the sales growth forecast as to what systems you have in place and will need to cope with the extra number of orders. Also what changes will be needed to your infrastructure, what upgrades in technology you will need, and the extra manpower needed to cope with running the business during your scaling period.

Suppliers

A vital part of scaling your business is your suppliers. You must be able to trust that your suppliers are able to scale with you and that you will not find yourself in the middle of your scaling operation having to deal with a supplier who cannot keep up with your increased orders. Make absolutely sure your supplier can keep up, especially if your scaling involves custom products or new products on the market. Should you have doubts about the supplier's ability, it is wise to search for a new supplier or a backup supplier.

When you start scaling communicate with your suppliers, you bring them into the picture. Suppliers are totally aware of the benefits your scaling will bring to their own business. They would prefer that you stay loyal to them, so negotiate the best prices for the products you are scaling. If you have built a solid business relationship with your suppliers, the majority of them will be open to negotiations.

Support Staff

As your business grows and orders increase, you need support staff as you will reach a stage where you can no longer handle the orders coming, customer queries and placing orders on your own. No business can afford to have a bad relationship with clients and especially new clients. You need to have a competent person or persons in place who will be able to help you deal with customer queries and communicate with and place orders with your suppliers.

A cost-effective way to have the needed support staff in place is to outsource by hiring a virtual assistant or virtual assistants for your specific business requirements. You can train and introduce your virtual assistant to your suppliers and you do not have to spend money on extras such as office space and equipment. This means you can use the money in your cash safety net for other needs within your business.

Technology and Automation

Automation is top of the list for the smooth running of any dropshipping company, and doubly so during the process of scaling. There simply is no time to do tasks manually as it is too time consuming, leaving you with little or no time to concentrate on the many extra tasks that need to be done to scale successfully.

Two forms of automation to put in place before you start scaling is to automate order fulfilment and auto order tracking. These to automation options keep orders being placed going and keep customers happy as they can track the progress of their orders. Tracking is especially beneficial when you are dealing with first time customers who may be uncomfortable dealing with a company they do not really know.

Make sure that you integrate as many of your systems as possible to prevent communications problems. The more unintegrated systems you have, the higher the chances are that the systems will not function well together, so prevent problems further along the line by integrating your systems to the greatest extent possible.

CHAPTER 13

Growing Your Business to $10,000+ / Month

Note that Facebook is the biggest social media channel there is. However, it can be costly. The next place you want to setup your marketing is on Twitter. It is cheaper and you can always start for free.

Finally, you can move on to Instagram and Pinterest maybe after you have seen the numbers and results in either Facebook or Twitter. Check how many conversions you're getting, how much web traffic is generated (how many people visit your site because of your ads), and see how many leads are generated (how many new accounts, add to carts, and checkouts are made).

Check if your market is on Facebook or if it is on Twitter. Remember that these are pay per click methods. You will have to pay these platforms for the amount of traffic they are able to generate on your dropshipping store.

Note that Twitter is seen by many ecommerce marketers as a very reliable social media platform as far as conversion is concerned. According to one study, about 52% of its users tend to buy products that are advertised there. On top of that they have 5 times more customer engagement, which increases your chances of conversion.

https://www.webfx.com/blog/social-media/why-twitter-matters-to-marketing-infographic/

However, that doesn't mean that you should forget about Facebook and the other social media channels. Facebook actually reports some pretty good ROI for digital marketers. Consider the following:

Scaling Your Business

Scaling your business means that you need to move forward and grow. At first you will be a one man team. If you can manage that then it will be great to do it by yourself. There won't be that many tasks to do at first.

All you need to do is to create your customer personas, do your research, setup your dropshipping site, register your business (i.e. sole proprietorship at first), pick and post your products, advertise in your selected medium, and then watch the analytics.

You need to determine where your customers are actually coming from. That will take a while. You will also need to craft ad campaigns, which means creating images, videos, slogans, and what not.

To scale your business you need to do the following:

- Add complimentary products
- Use the power of email lists

- Increase your market spend
- Hire a virtual assistant (you can't do it all your own anymore)
- Go multichannel

Add Complimentary Products

Find out which of your listed products sell. You will then go back to Amazon or some other online retailing portal (like eBay for instance or a competing dropshipping site).

Look for your product there. You're not the only one selling it, remember? If you're product is unique then you should look for similar product. For instance, if you're selling waterproof Bluetooth speakers, then look for Bluetooth speakers that are also waterproof and are about the same price.

And then look at the "People who viewed this item also viewed" part of those product pages. Another section is the "often bought together" section that shows which other products were also bought with that Bluetooth speaker.

That will give you a good idea of the complimentary products that you can sell on your site as well.

You can also brainstorm things too. Think of other possible products that will complement your product. If you're selling a Vitamin D supplement, your customers might also be interested in Calcium and Magnesium supplements as well.

Why? Well, you need a balance of all of these three nutrients so that you can get the most of the benefits you get from all of them. Do your due diligence—do some research.

You can also just create a different offer—a competing product perhaps. And then see if people buy that instead or just head off to their own choice of complimentary product. The goal is to make people make their move and observe how what they do on your website. Make use of the analytics tools provided to you from the different social media channels and Google as well.

You're Going to Get Busy with the Problems

Here's a bit of fair warning. As your sales increase expect to get more returns and customer complaints. Big Hint: deal with it as fast as you can and as efficiently as you can or else your reputation will suffer.

Returns

Customers will return products for one reason or another. You should immediately check the return policy on that product (30 day or 45 day money back guarantees etc.). Base your next move on that policy provided by your supplier.

Chargebacks

Sometimes you will get chargeback notifs. More often than not a chargeback is actually fraudulent. However, the bank won't give you a lot of time so you better act quickly. You need to provide proof that you actually delivered the goods. Evidence come in the form of packing slip, tracking information, and the exact order that was made.

Shipping Type

Most dropshippers will offer free shipping and just work the cost into the list price they display on their online store. How are they able to do that? Well, they opt for flat rate shipping. It's the same charge for all items you sell.

But that is not always available. Sometimes you will have to use per type rates especially if the item being shipped is heavier or larger. If you're shipping larger packages your best carrier options are FedEx and UPS. They give better rates.

If you are usually shipping smaller items then USPS is the go to carrier. They can charge less than $5 per package.

Customer Support

Expect to do some customer support yourself at certain times. A lot of dropshippers use support software to help them manage customer complaints and provide support options. Here are the top 3 choices for many dropshippers:

- Desk (operated by Salesforce)
- Help Scout (go to option for personalized service and it has a pretty good support ticket system)
- Zendesk (has lots of pricing options—great for beginners with smaller budgets).

Email Lists

Email lists are still a staple for ecommerce. If you already have your own website and your own dropshipping site then it makes sense to create an email list. You can offer discount coupon codes, product guides, brochures, create discount events or anything that you can provide for free in exchange for your customer's email address.

You should also indicate that you will be sending them promotional items on their emails when you ask for their email addresses.

You also shouldn't pepper your subscribers with emails every day. That will be annoying. You should schedule your emails like maybe once or twice a week. Email them whenever you have a sale coming up.

Here are some of the types of emails that you might want to send your customers:

- Welcome email
- Help email
- Answers to inquiries
- Unexpected freebie email
- Newsletters
- Important events email

You will want to use an email marketing service later on. It's easy to send out those emails to 25 or even 50 of your close friends and relatives. But as your customer base grows and as your website gains popularity, expect your list of emails to grow to the hundreds (or even thousands).

That is why you need the help of an email marketing service to help manage all of that. Mailchimp is the popular email marketing brand out there. However, there are other alternatives such as Benchmark, MailerLite, GetResponse, and others. Check out their rates and see which ones fit your budget.

You will also want to spend time to learn more about email marketing. Again it's a huge subject and it can't be covered comprehensively in this book.

Increase Your Marketing Spend

After a lot of fine tuning (i.e. mistakes and blunders) you will find out the best practices and the best products for your dropshipping store. You will then need to increase your marketing spend.

That means increasing your marketing budget. You already know your niche and your market. Now it's time to get more sales and in order to do that you need more aggressive marketing ergo more funds spent on ads and analytics monitoring.

Hiring a Virtual Assistant

As your success grows your market grows. That also means you will get more customer complaints and experience more problems. You will end up getting so busy it can drive you crazy.

That means you have grown your business to a point where you can't do it on your own anymore. Then you have to delegate some of the repetitive tasks of your business to someone else and focus on the important stuff—marketing, sales, and advertising.

This is where a virtual assistant can come into play. Alternatively you can hire someone in the neighborhood but that might entail some legalities which can drain more of your funds. Maybe you can do that later when your business has grown a little bit bigger.

For now a virtual assistant who will work part time will have to do. You can delegate the following tasks to a VA:

- Graphic design
- SEO work
- Website maintenance
- Creating blog posts
- Writing newsletters
- Updating inventory
- Processing invoices
- Social media management
- Customer service

So, where do you hire your prospective VA? There are lots of platforms where Vas post their professional profiles. You can hire them from Upwork, Zirtual, or Freelancer. Those are the top 3 nowadays but there are others too.

Note that sooner or later you will need to assemble a team or several teams. Some VAs and in house employees will be in charge of marketing. Some will be tasked with customer service (you'll need help dealing with hundreds if not thousands of customers), and others will be tasked with site management, product research, and other tasks as well.

CHAPTER 14

Social Media Approach in Dropshipping

A successful business does well marketing on public streets but the truth is since we are entering a new age of electronic future businesses must make haste for their change if they haven't gotten to it yet. This next change is to discover the new world of social media marketing. You are going to be reaching out online in many different ways. If there has been any previous advertisement experience had for the Business then one knows the power the word of mouth can bring.

Having social interactions with others build a great rapport with the individuals engaged. This kind of behavior is going to promote the global presence that the e-commerce shop has. Bringing in social media to an already online and trending topic is going to make with e-commerce a perfect pair. A business might have more than half of their following on a social media scale and thus in great odds will also make it easier to combine them into some good business marketing.

Bring the business to the front lines and where more than half the customers are; that's online. The web is going to be a strong motivator for content you are going to design your product line. Release a post about your new inventory and be descriptive when you tell the world that is going to pop and be a strong reminder to the visitors why they

120

are going to visit your shop and ultimately why they will buy. Get started now and try making a social media account if you do not have one already.

There are tons of providers and many of them you will be able to market your business with. Create a login and finish editing the personal information on the account and everything that the business will be displaying to the public. Make the business account look nice and professional and it will attract business-like followers ready to see your catalog. Choose a provider that fits your needs or open two or many accounts to see which is going to work best for the business. The business owner may choose one social media outlet over another and this could give the business presence edge.

The only way to tell the right fit is to just jump right in and start designing. Social media has strong sources of the population that are willing to third-party market and this is why it's important to establish a bond with the community that surrounds. It can city-based or global to give back in many ways as long as you make the connection with your audience. Make their time worthwhile since they are spending so much online searching. Supply an online incentive that will encourage your audience to come back and share the content with other friends and family that are with them on these accounts. Find important partners that can also give you mentions and that will give you credible posts about the business you run and for many to see.

The question is can the e-commerce website survive from only social media marketing. This is not going to be a likely route because the only option the business has could lose it and have nothing left for support.

If the company only dedicated their marketing budget to social media marketing, they are going to see the expensive cost burn through the budget quickly. Popularity is so important when it comes to running an efficiently visited shop but the company needs to take advantage of its capabilities to obtain followers from the social media sites that they could also be using, some of them even being free.

The more popularity you have the more profitable the business can be. The business can create very engaging motives towards their audience and they could attract more and more attention to the sites that are trickling into the shop daily. Keep gaining more followers and see what this popularity can do for the business.

Facebook Ads

Facebook ads are great and they are for any age range with a company structure. With Facebook as a company can market themselves from the bottom up and with little to no cost at all. Running Facebook ads can become costly if there is no following audience to broadcast to. If the company has no following on their web-sites then they are going to be paying money for company promotion and not for product promotion depending on how far we have gotten already.

These social ads are great because it engages thousands of people together for a common focus on the marketplace and this creates a strong playing field for posting products on any page. A company can pay for personalized ads that are going to air for the community to see sponsored posts on their pages and feeds so that they cleverly run into company products posted for great values. These advertisements cost the company upfront but they will also give great exposure to the presence of the shop.

The shop can post an ad about its new items or maybe marked down items that the company has extra inventory of. If the company can make an ad about the marked down items that are full in the inventory ware-house then products can be efficiently moved off of the warehouse shelves and into new revenue that is going to have the company break even with its assets. There has to be a balanced routine when it comes to paying for Facebook ads because not only can they get pricey but there will also be other ads that bring competition to the playing board.

It is in the best interest of the company to know exactly when to place an ad on the market. The company is going to need to be ready for any turnover and sales to skyrocket if necessary because if there is the right product niche the success is going to come pouring out. Customize ads with the company logo and titles that entice the customers to come on in and visit for the new sales. There is going to be opportunities to make a catalog or a flip advertisement and get creative with the cover flow when putting up an advertisement for the week.

Advertise on a good schedule so that none of the customers see the posts as spam and give the audience a chance to respond to the advertisement and give feedback about the current promotion. Utilize these ads when holidays come around and make an advertisement that speaks out above news in the Facebook place. This Facebook marketplace is going to create a level opportunity to see your posts and engage with the shop site that you like to involve in the posts. Ads can also be placed on the Facebook marketplace and this could include single items or bulk items.

This is a not usually the case because there are at times selling restrictions under certain sites but with Facebook ads this allows the company to list any variety of products. The company will be able to list products that can be sold as common goods or rare goods that are even handmade and at a limited source. Take advantage of the market diversity within Facebook because it will create a great opportunity to post and post again even when the product may not have sold the first week. If the product does not sell the first week through a Facebook ad markup the price and make the product bio look spiffier.

When the customers see that ad again they will have a new take on it and they will dedicate more time to considering visiting the shop site and picking out something that encouraged them to get there. With Facebook ads, it will be easier and easier for the average product supplier to have a global reach for the line in their shop. Global diversity is important so that every market genre can be tapped into and the company can take full advantage of selling their products to everyone around the world never missing a sale.

Google Adwords

With Google Adwords, there is going to be great diversity in search engines to bring plenty of crowds to the consumer website. With Google, Adwords google is going to place ads for the company on several landing servers and it is going to create ad space for all sites that are affected. Adwords is going to display ads for the company that relates to the company's mission or its makeup so that when someone is shopping or researching a site low and behold there will be an ad for the company and its product. This company ad is going to replace any space that may not have had an ad in the first place and this will create brand marketing for anyone who sees this ad.

Adwords control the ads that individuals see when they conduct searches like google searches for a specific product. This search is going to bring up many trending topics and depending on how much money the company decided to spend with AdWords the trending topic could the shop on a seasonal weekend. If the company is just starting Adwords is going to make a great opener for a company that has not built any brand advertisement. Lead a great advertising campaign by setting some money aside and spending it on advertisements every quarter to create a better-defined presence online.

This is going to maximize the reach the company makes on all of the audiences and this is going to ramp up production for any customers that have not seen or purchased from the shop yet. If product awareness can be brought to attention for the viewers all at once there could be a high spike of customers that come in to purchase all at once and this could send the company into a new stratosphere of sales. One of the main consistencies is the crowd flow and the amount of advertisement money spent which could be with Google Adwords.

CONCLUSION

Dropshipping has been around for nearly two decades, yet it still proves to be a highly effective business model for turning a profit online. These days, if you want to be a dropshipper there is plenty of information out there about how you can get started and what you need to do in order to turn your business into a success. The key for you is to ensure that the information you are reading is relevant and high-quality so that you can find yourself amongst the top earners in this industry.

I hope that through reading Dropshipping for Beginners you were able to identify a strong approach for you to get into dropshipping and earn a profit. By giving you some insight as to what this industry is and a clear strategy for how you can get started and grow your business, I hope that you now feel confident in generating your own success. If you really want to make the most out of this information, you need to be ready to apply it with consistency and confidence every step of the way so that you can generate a huge income through your business.

The next step after reading this book is to research what industries are the most successful for dropshipping and then find yourself a niche that you can build in. After that, you can begin to create your brand and grow your business through developing an online presence for you to reach your customers with.

Make sure that you start small and grow out, as this is the best way to ensure that you test your niche first so that you can validate its profitability. If your results are promising, you can use this information to help you increase your sales and grow your business out even further. As well, don't forget to check out my other titles like Amazon FBA so that you can further grow your knowledge in this industry! Knowing exactly what you can do to grow your business through strong sales channels is going to help you get your name out there and maximize your success in this industry.

You also need to make sure that you pay close attention to the tips and advice that I have given you, as this information can help you succeed even faster. The information I have provided you with here is intended to help you quickly grow beyond many beginners' mistakes and challenges, whereby you can step into mastering your dropshipping business right from day one. Avoid underestimating this advice, as it truly can help set you apart and guarantee your success in the industry!

CPSIA information can be obtained
at www.ICGtesting.com
Printed in the USA
LVHW050047091220
673659LV00034B/917